T0334421

THE FUTURES BOND BASIS

Second Edition

The Securities & Investment Institute

Mission Statement:

> *To set standards of professional excellence and integrity for the investment and securities industry, providing qualifications and promoting the highest level of competence to our members, other individuals and firms.*

The Securities and Investment Institute is the UK's leading professional and membership body for practitioners in the securities and investment industry, with more than 16,000 members with an increasing number working outside the UK. It is also the major examining body for the industry, with a full range of qualifications aimed at people entering and working in it. More than 30,000 examinations are taken annually in more than 30 countries.

You can contact us through our website *www.sii.org.uk*

Our membership believes that keeping up to date is central to professional development. We are delighted to endorse the Wiley/SII publishing partnership and recommend this series of books to our members and all those who work in the industry.

Ruth Martin
Managing Director

THE FUTURES BOND BASIS

Second Edition

Moorad Choudhry

JOHN WILEY & SONS, LTD

Published in 2006 by John Wiley & Sons Ltd, The Atrium, Southern Gate, Chichester,
West Sussex PO19 8SQ, England
Telephone (+44) 1243 779777
Email (for orders and customer service enquiries): cs-books@wiley.co.uk
Visit our Home Page on www.wiley.com

Copyright © 2006 Moorad Choudhry

All Rights Reserved. No part of this publication may be reproduced, stored in a retrieval
system or transmitted in any form or by any means, electronic, mechanical, photocopying,
recording, scanning or otherwise, except under the terms of the Copyright, Designs and
Patents Act 1988 or under the terms of a licence issued by the Copyright Licensing Agency
Ltd, 90 Tottenham Court Road, London W1T 4LP, UK, without the permission in writing of
the Publisher. Requests to the Publisher should be addressed to the Permissions Department,
John Wiley & Sons Ltd, The Atrium, Southern Gate, Chichester, West Sussex PO19 8SQ,
England, or emailed to permreq@wiley.co.uk, or faxed to (+44) 1243 770620

Designations used by companies to distinguish their products are often claimed as trademarks.
All brand names and product names used in this book are trade names, trademarks or registered
trademarks of their respective owners. The Publisher is not associated with any product or
vendor mentioned in this book.

This publication is designed to provide accurate and authoritative information in regard to
the subject matter covered. It is sold on the understanding that the Publisher is not engaged
in rendering professional services. If professional advice or other expert assistance is
required, the services of a competent professional should be sought.

The views, thoughts and opinions expressed in this book are those of Moorad Choudhry in his
individual private capacity and should not be taken to be the views of KBC Financial Products or
KBC Bank N.V., or of Moorad Choudhry as an employee, officer or representative of KBC
Financial Products or KBC Bank N.V.

Other Wiley Editorial Offices

John Wiley & Sons, Inc., 111 River Street, Hoboken, NJ 07030, USA

Jossey-Bass, 989 Market Street, San Francisco, CA 94103-1741, USA

Wiley-VCH Verlag GmbH, Boschstr. 12, D-69469 Weinheim, Germany

John Wiley & Sons Australia Ltd, 42 McDougall Street, Milton, Queensland 4064, Australia

John Wiley & Sons (Asia) Pte Ltd, 2 Clementi Loop #02-01, Jin Xing Distripark, Singapore 129809

John Wiley & Sons Canada Ltd, 22 Worcester Road, Etobicoke, Ontario, Canada M9W 1L1

Wiley also publishes its books in a variety of electronic formats. Some content that appears
in print may not be available in electronic books.

British Library Cataloguing in Publication Data

A catalogue record for this book is available from the British Library

ISBN-13 978-0-470-02589-5 (PB)
ISBN-10 0-470-02589-1 (PB)

Project management by Originator, Gt Yarmouth, Norfolk (typeset in 12/16pt Trump Mediaeval).

This book is printed on acid-free paper responsibly manufactured from sustainable forestry
in which at least two trees are planted for each one used for paper production.

To Alan Fulling ...
whose impact on my life has been much greater than
he could possibly imagine

CONTENTS

....

Appendices

PREFACE

This book is aimed at all those with an involvement in cash bond and bond futures markets. This includes traders and salespersons in investment banks, as well as fund managers. Others such as post-graduate students in finance may also find the contents useful. The first edition of this book was a (hopefully!) succinct and accessible look at the government bond futures basis. The concept of the basis can be applied in any financial market, not just that of government bonds, and refers essentially to the price differential between cash and derivative (or synthetic) versions of the same asset. The second edition of the book builds on this and also introduces more background on futures contracts as well as more illustrations. The expanded approach should help to answer the question of 'What exactly is the basis?' and 'How does one trade the basis?'. We also introduce in this edition an accessible account of the Z-spread, which is a bond yield spread used in relative value analysis. This is becoming increasingly relevant in an era of credit derivative basis trading, which, however, must remain the preserve of another book. Government bond markets do not exist in isolation, and while there are certainly dedicated desks of traders in banks whose sole job it is to trade the government basis, some of our readers will be interested in the interaction between risk-free and credit-risky markets. But we remain true to our original purpose, hence we place the introduction to bond spreads in an Appendix! This second edition also provides, for reference purposes, background information on repurchase agreements or *repo*. The most important element in a basis trade is its financing, which is carried out in the repo market. Hence, this additional detail is again placed out-of-the-way in an Appendix.

Government bond futures contracts, traded on an exchange and representing a very liquid product, are a key component of the global bond markets. The nominal value of bonds represented by daily trading in the futures markets far exceeds the actual nominal value of the cash bond market itself. The difference between the price of a cash bond and its implied price as given by a futures contract is the *basis*. The basis has a significant impact on the use of bond futures for both hedging and speculative purposes. Given its importance, it is vital that market participants have a clear understanding both of the basis itself as well as its dynamics.

The cash government bond market is the cornerstone of the debt capital markets, and provides the benchmark rate of return against which all other asset returns are priced and assessed. This reflects, in advanced economies, its status as a risk-free market. The futures market is arguably as important as the cash market, as futures contracts are the main hedging and risk management tool used by cash bond traders and investors. As such, futures contracts are essential to maintaining liquidity and market transparency.

Government cash and derivatives markets exist in a symbiotic relationship. Hence, it becomes important to understand the relationship between the two markets. The objective of this book is to address key questions on the exact definition of the basis, how the basis behaves in practice and how one should analyse the basis if one wishes to trade it. As we mentioned at the start, the concept of the basis exists for all derivative contracts. The price differential between a barrel of crude oil and the same barrel represented by a futures contract is also the basis. Generally, the basis for an oil contract should reflect the difference in cost between delivering a barrel of oil now or storing and delivering it later – there will be storage costs to cover. The difference with a bond contract is that, unlike with crude oil, holding a government bond actually produces income, provided that the yield on the bond is above the bond's financing (or repo) rate, so the basis for a bond futures may actually be negative. This reflects that the price of the bond implied by the futures contract may be lower than the cash price – this flies in the face of logic but is easily explained, as we shall see.

We have already defined the basis then – the price differential between the cash asset price and the asset price for future delivery implied by the futures contract. For a bond future, the basis is the price difference between the cash bond and the futures contract, but adjusted by the contract's *conversion factor*. The conversion factor equates the futures contract to the bond, because, as we shall see, there are a number of different bonds all represented by the same contract. Using conversion factors in essence means we are able to assess all cash bonds on a like-by-like basis (no pun intended!).

What about trading the basis? It is a form of arbitrage trading, in this case the simultaneous trading of cash bonds and bond futures contracts to exploit a perceived mis-pricing in one or both instruments. If we 'buy the basis' we are buying the bond and selling the future, while 'selling the basis' is the simultaneous sale of the cash bond and purchase of the bond future. These days, market makers will quote you a price that enables one to execute both sides of the trade at once. This eliminates the need to 'leg into' the trade, which is when one side, either cash or future, is transacted first. This can be a risky approach because the market may well have moved before the other leg can be executed, which means the trade is off-side right from the start and has no chance, or little chance, of making a profit.

We will explore this further in the following chapters.

CONTENT OF THE BOOK

The objective of this book is to describe and explain the basis in non-technical terms. We do this by taking examples from the United Kingdom gilt market, although the basic principles will be applicable in any bond futures market. As such, we consider:

- the futures contracts themselves, including contract specifications and the concept of the cheapest-to-deliver;
- price and delivery data for a sample of gilt contracts;
- the drivers of the basis and its dynamics;
- the mechanics of basis trading;
- a detailed explanation of gross and net basis, and the implied repo rate.

We wish to provide an introductory description and analysis of the futures bond basis; readers who wish to investigate the bond and derivatives markets to greater depth may wish to consult the author's book *The Bond and Money Markets: Strategy, Trading, Analysis*, published by Butterworth Heinemann (2001) or his later book *Fixed Income Markets: Instruments, Applications, Mathematics*, published by John Wiley & Sons (2004).

Further information on the fixed income markets is available at the fixed income research website:

www.yieldcurve.com

Comments on the text are welcome and should be sent to the author care of John Wiley & Sons.

ABOUT THE AUTHOR

Moorad Choudhry is Head of Treasury at KBC Financial Products in London. He traded government bond futures contracts while employed as a gilts trader at Hambros Bank Limited and ABN Amro Hoare Govett Sterling Bonds Limited.

Dr Choudhry is a Visiting Professor at the Department of Economics, London Metropolitan University, a Visiting Research Fellow at the ICMA Centre, University of Reading, a Senior Fellow at the Centre for Mathematical Trading and Finance, Cass Business School, and a Fellow of the Securities and Investment Institute.

Chapter

1

....

BOND FUTURES CONTRACTS

A widely used trading and risk management instrument in the bond markets is the government bond futures contract. This is an exchange-traded standardised contract that fixes the price today at which a specified quantity and quality of a bond will be delivered at a date during the expiry month of the futures contract. Unlike short-term interest rate futures, which only require cash settlement, bond futures require the actual physical delivery of a bond when they are settled. They are in this respect more akin to commodity futures contracts, which are also (in theory) physically settled.

In this first chapter we review bond futures contracts and their use for trading and hedging purposes.

1.1   INTRODUCTION

A *futures contract* is an agreement between two counterparties that fixes the terms of an exchange that will take place between them at some future date. They are standardised agreements as opposed to 'over-the-counter' or *OTC* ones, as they are traded on an exchange, so they are also referred to as *exchange-traded futures*. In the UK financial futures are traded on *LIFFE*, the London International Financial Futures Exchange which opened in 1982. LIFFE is the biggest financial futures exchange in Europe in terms of volume of contracts traded. There are four classes of contract traded on LIFFE: short-term interest rate contracts, long-term interest rate contracts (bond futures), currency contracts and stock index contracts.

Bond futures contracts, which are an important part of the bond markets, are used for hedging and speculative purposes. Most futures contracts on exchanges around the world trade at 3-month maturity intervals, with maturity dates fixed at March, June, September and December each year. This includes the contracts traded on LIFFE. Therefore, at pre-set times during the year a contract for each of these months will *expire*, and a final *settlement* price is determined for it. The further out one goes the less liquid the trading is in that contract. It is normal to see liquid trading only in the *front* month contract (the current contract, so that if we are trading in April 2005 the front month is the June 2005 future), and possibly one or two of the next contracts, for most bond futures contracts. The liquidity of contracts diminishes the further one trades out in the maturity range.

When a party establishes a position in a futures contract, it can either run this position to maturity or close out the position between trade date and maturity. If a position is closed out the party will have either a profit or loss to book. If a position is held until maturity, the party who is long futures will take delivery of the underlying asset (bond) at the settlement price; the party who is short futures will deliver the underlying asset. This is referred to as *physical settlement* or sometimes, confusingly, as *cash settlement*. There is no counterparty risk associated with trading exchange-traded futures, because of the role of the *clearing house*, such as the London Clearing House (*LCH*). This is the body through which contracts are settled. A clearing house acts as the buyer to all contracts sold on the exchange, and the seller to all contracts that are bought. So in the London market the LCH acts as the counterparty to all transactions, so that settlement is effectively guaranteed. The LCH requires all exchange participants to deposit margin with it, a cash sum that is the cost of conducting business (plus brokers' commissions). The size of the margin depends on the size of a party's net *open* position in contracts (an open position is a position in a contract that is held overnight and not closed out). There are two types of margin, *maintenance margin* and *variation margin*. Maintenance margin is the minimum level required to be held at the clearing house; the level is set by the exchange. Variation margin is the additional amount that must be deposited to cover any trading losses and as the size of the net open positions increases. Note that this is not like margin in, say, a repo transaction. Margin in repo is a safeguard against a drop in value of collateral that has been supplied against a loan of cash. The margin deposited at a futures exchange clearing house acts essentially as 'good faith' funds, required to provide comfort to the exchange that the futures trader is able to satisfy the obligations of the futures contract.

1.1.1 Contract specifications

We have noted that futures contracts traded on an exchange are standardised. This means that each contract represents exactly the same commodity, and it cannot be tailored to meet individual customer requirements. In this section we describe two very liquid and commonly traded contracts, starting with the US Treasury bond

Table 1.1 CBOT US T-bond futures contract specification.

Unit of trading	US T-bond with notional value of $100,000 and a coupon of 6%
Deliverable grades	US T-bonds with a minimum maturity of 15 years from first day of delivery month
Delivery months	March, June, September, December
Delivery date	Any business day during the delivery month
Last trading day	12:00 noon, 7th business day before last business day of delivery month
Quotation	Per cent of par expressed as points and thirty-seconds of a point – e.g., 108 – 16 is 108 16/32 or 108.50
Minimum price movement	1/32
Tick value	$31.25
Trading hours	07:20–14:00 (trading pit) 17:20–20:05 22:30–06:00 hours (screen trading)

Source: CBOT.

(*T-bond*) contract traded on the Chicago Board of Trade (*CBOT*). The details of this contract are given in Table 1.1.

The terms of this contract relate to a US T-bond with a minimum maturity of 15 years and a *notional* coupon of 8%. A futures contract specifies a notional coupon to prevent delivery and liquidity problems that would arise if there was shortage of bonds with exactly the coupon required, or if one market participant purchased a large proportion of all the bonds in issue with the required coupon. For exchange-traded futures, a short future can deliver any bond that fits the maturity criteria specified in the contract terms. Of course, a long future would like to deliver a high-coupon bond with significant accrued interest, while the short future would want to deliver a low-coupon bond with low interest accrued. In fact, this issue does not arise because of the way the *invoice amount* (the amount paid by the long future to purchase the bond) is calculated. The invoice amount on the expiry date is given as equation (1.1):

$$Inv_{amt} = P_{fut} \times CF + AI \qquad (1.1)$$

where Inv_{amt} = Invoice amount;
P_{fut} = Price of the futures contract;
CF = Conversion factor;
AI = Bond accrued interest.

Any bond that meets the maturity specifications of the futures contract is said to be in the *delivery basket*, the group of bonds that are eligible to be delivered into the futures contract. Every bond in the delivery basket will have its own *conversion factor*, which is used to equalise coupon and accrued interest differences of all the delivery bonds. The exchange will announce the conversion factor for each bond before trading in a contract begins; the conversion factor for a bond will change over time, but remains fixed for one individual contract. That is, if a bond has a conversion factor of 1.091 252, this will remain fixed for the life of the contract. If a contract specifies a bond with a notional coupon of 7%, then the conversion factor will be less than 1.0 for bonds with a coupon lower than 7% and higher than 1.0 for bonds with a coupon higher than 7%. A formal definition of conversion factor is given below.

Conversion factor

The conversion factor (or *price factor*) gives the price of an individual cash bond such that its yield to maturity on the delivery day of the futures contract is equal to the notional coupon of the contract. The product of the conversion factor and the futures price is the forward price available in the futures market for that cash bond (plus the cost of funding, referred to as the gross basis). Each bond that is deliverable against the futures contract is given a conversion factor.

Although conversion factors equalise the yield on bonds, bonds in the delivery basket will trade at different yields, and for this reason they are not 'equal' at the time of delivery. Certain bonds will be cheaper than others, and one bond will be the *cheapest-to-deliver* (*CTD*) bond. The cheapest-to-deliver bond is the one that gives the greatest return from a strategy of buying a bond and simultaneously selling the futures contract, and then closing out positions on the expiry of the contract. This so-called *cash-and-carry trading* is actively pursued by proprietary trading desks in banks. If a contract is purchased and then held to maturity the buyer will receive, via the exchange's clearing house, the cheapest-to-deliver gilt. Traders sometimes try to exploit arbitrage price differentials between the future and the cheapest-to-deliver gilt, which is *basis trading*.

The mathematical calculation of the conversion factor for the gilt future is given in Appendix 1.A.

Conversion factors are set by the Exchange at the inception of the contract and stay unchanged for the life of the contract. They are unique to each bond and to each delivery month. Table 1.2 shows the conversion factor for the deliverable basket of gilts during 2004–2005. These are gilts that were in the deliverable basket for the Dec05 contract. If a bond has a coupon higher than the notional coupon of the contract, its conversion factor will be higher than 1, while the bonds with a coupon lower than the contract notional coupon will have a conversion factor lower than 1. This can also be seen from Table 1.2. Note how the conversion factor pulls towards 1 the nearer to expiry the deliverable bond gets. In the case of bonds with coupon below the notional coupon, this means the conversion factor steadily increases with each new futures contract, while the opposite happens with bonds whose coupon is higher than the notional coupon.

Table 1.2 Conversion factors over time for deliverable gilts i▮

Gilt	Contract		
	GU4 (Sep04)	GZ4 (Dec04)	GH5 (Mar05
8% 2013	1.138 279 2	1.135 309 8	—
5% 2014	0.925 536 1	0.926 810 5	0.928 300 5
8% 2015	1.161 926 3	1.159 557 6	1.156 832 7
4.75% 2015	0.900 301 3	0.901 826 7	0.903 558 4
8.75% 2017	1.245 543 9	1.242 273 2	1.239 273 8

Source: Bloomberg.

Conversion factors are NOT hedge ratios and should not be used as such. The primary use of the conversion factor is as a definition of the basis. When the conversion factor is used as a ratio to combine bonds and futures, a change in the bond's basis will generate profit for the arbitrage trader, irrespective of whether the basis moved to a change in bond price or futures price. The potential profit is also not market directional; that is, it is not relevant whether a rise or fall in bond or futures price has caused a change in the basis.

We summarise the contract specification of the long gilt futures contract traded on LIFFE in Table 1.3. There is also a medium gilt contract on LIFFE, which was introduced in 1998 (having been discontinued in the early 1990s). This trades a notional 5-year gilt, with eligible gilts being those of 4–7 years' maturity.

Figures 1.1A and 1.2 show Bloomberg screen DES for the US Treasury long bond and UK gilt contracts,

e delivery basket for Dec05 contract, during 2004–2005.

ilt	Contract		
	GM5 (Jun05)	GU5 (Sep05)	GZ5 (Dec05)
% 2013	—	—	—
% 2014	0.929 611 3	0.931 150 5	0.932 508 9
% 2015	1.154 344 8	1.151 496 6	1.148 973 4
.75% 2015	0.905 126 7	0.906 916 4	0.908 540 7
.75% 2017	1.235 810 8	1.232 586 5	1.229 125 0

Table 1.3 LIFFE long gilt future contract specification.

Unit of trading	UK gilt bond having a face value of £100,000, a notional coupon of 6% and a notional maturity of 10 years (changed from contract value of £50,000 from the September 1998 contract)
Deliverable grades	UK gilts with a maturity ranging from $8\frac{3}{4}$ to 13 years from the 1st day of the delivery month (changed from 10–15 years from the December 1998 contract)
Delivery months	March, June, September, December
Delivery date	Any business day during the delivery month
Last trading day	11:00 hours, 2 business days before last business day of delivery month
Quotation	Per cent of par expressed as points and hundredths of a point – for example, 114.56 (changed from ticks and 1/32nds of a point, as in 114-17 meaning 114 17/32 or 114.531 25, from the June 1998 contract)
Minimum price movement	0.01 of one point (one tick)
Tick value	£10
Trading hours	08:00–18:00 hours. All trading conducted electronically on LIFFE CONNECT platform

Source: LIFFE.

respectively. The Treasury is 'listed', if one can say this, on CBOT but can of course be traded 24 hours a day on Globex, Simex and other exchanges.

Figure 1.1B shows page CTM from Bloomberg, a list of the current long bond contracts as at 1 November 2005. The 'front month' contract is the Dec05 future, trading at 112-03. The screen also shows trading volume data,

Figure 1.1A Bloomberg page DES showing contract characteristics for US Treasury long bond futures contract.

© Bloomberg L.P. Used with permission. Visit *www.bloomberg.com*

we can see that the 'open interest' is 577,046 lots. Open interest is the number of contracts that have been traded and whose positions have been run overnight; that is, they were traded and are not yet closed out.

1.2 FUTURES PRICING

We now introduce the first principles behind the pricing of a futures contract. In practice, cash markets are now priced off derivatives markets, reflecting the greater liquidity of the latter. However, understanding the theory allows for a greater understanding of the nature of the contract itself.

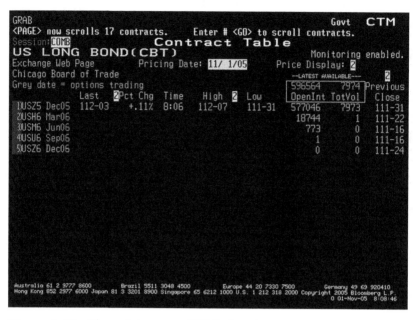

Figure 1.1B   Bloomberg page CTM showing current contract price and volume data for US Treasury long bond futures contract, 1 November 2005.

© Bloomberg L.P. Used with permission. Visit *www.bloomberg.com*

1.2.1   Theoretical principle

Although it may not appear so on first trading, floor trading on a futures exchange is probably the closest one gets to an example of the economist's perfect and efficient market. The immediacy and liquidity of the market will ensure that at virtually all times the price of any futures contract reflects fair value. In essence, because a futures contract represents an underlying asset, albeit a synthetic one, its price cannot differ from the actual cash market price of the asset itself. This is because the market sets futures prices such that they are arbitrage-free. We can illustrate this with a hypothetical

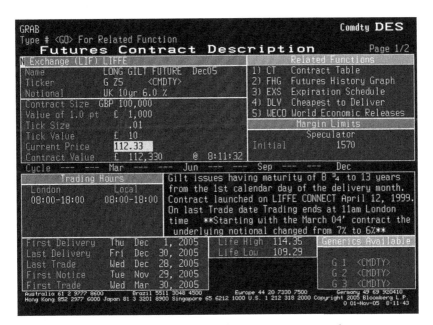

Figure 1.2 Bloomberg page DES showing contract characteristics for long gilt futures contract.

© Bloomberg L.P. Used with permission. Visit *www.bloomberg.com*

example. Let us say that the benchmark 10-year bond, with a coupon of 8%, is trading at par. This bond is the underlying asset represented by the long bond futures contract; the front month contract expires in precisely 3 months. If we also say that the 3-month London Inter-Bank Offer Rate (*LIBOR*) rate (here called the repo rate) is 6%, what is fair value for the front month futures contract? For the purpose of illustration let us start by assuming the futures price to be 105. We could carry out the following arbitrage-type trade:

- buy the bond for £100;
- simultaneously sell the future at £105;
- borrow £100 for 3 months at the repo rate of 6%.

As this is a leveraged trade we have borrowed the funds with which to buy the bond, and the loan is fixed at 3 months because we will hold the position to the futures contract expiry, which is in exactly 3 months' time. At expiry, as we are short futures we will deliver the underlying bond to the futures clearing house and close out the loan. This strategy will result in cash flows for us as shown below.

Futures settlement cash flows

Price received for bond = 105.00

Bond accrued = 2.00 (8% coupon for 3 months)

Total proceeds = 107.00

Loan cash flows

Repayment of principal = 100.00

Loan interest = 1.500 (6% repo rate for 3 months)

Total outlay = 101.50

The trade has resulted in a profit of £5.50, and this profit is guaranteed as we have traded the two positions simultaneously and held them both to maturity. We are not affected by subsequent market movements. The trade is an example of a pure arbitrage, which is risk-free. There is no cash outflow at the start of the trade because we borrowed the funds used to buy the bond. In essence, we have locked in the forward price of the bond by trading the future today, so that the final settlement price of the futures contract is irrelevant. If the situation described above were to occur in practice it would be very short-lived, precisely because arbitrageurs would buy the bond and sell the future to make this profit. This activity would force changes in the prices of both bond and future until the profit opportunity was removed.

So, in our illustration the price of the future was too high (and possibly the price of the bond was too low as well) and not reflecting fair value because the price of the synthetic asset was out of line with the cash asset.

What if the price of the future was too low? Let us imagine that the futures contract is trading at 95.00. We could then carry out the following trade:

- sell the bond at £100;
- simultaneously buy the future for £95;
- lend the proceeds of the short sale (£100) for 3 months at 6%.

This trade has the same procedure as the first one with no initial cash outflow, except that we have to cover the short position in the repo market, through which we invest the sale proceeds at the repo rate of 6%. After 3 months we are delivered a bond as part of the futures settlement, and this is used to close out our short position. How has our strategy performed?

Futures settlement cash flows

$$\text{Clean price of bond} = 95.00$$

$$\text{Bond accrued} = 2.00$$

$$\text{Total cash outflow} = 97.00$$

Loan cash flows

Principal on loan maturity = 100.00

Interest from loan = 1.500

Total cash inflow = 101.500

The profit of £4.50 is again a risk-free arbitrage profit. Of course, our hypothetical world has ignored considerations such as bid–offer spreads for the bond, future and repo rates, which would apply in the real world and impact on any trading strategy. Yet again, however, the futures price is out of line with the cash market and has provided opportunity for arbitrage profit.

Given the terms and conditions that apply in our example, there is one price for the futures contract at which no arbitrage profit opportunity is available. If we set the future price at 99.5, we would see that both trading strategies, buying the bond and selling the future or selling the bond and buying the future, yield a net cash flow of 0. There is no profit to be made from either strategy. So, at 99.5 the futures price is in line with the cash market, and it will only move as the cash market price moves; any other price will result in an arbitrage profit opportunity.

1.2.2   Arbitrage-free futures pricing

The previous section demonstrated how we can arrive at the fair value for a bond futures contract provided we have certain market information. The market mechanism and continuous trading will ensure that the fair price is achieved, as arbitrage profit opportunities are eliminated. We can determine the bond future's price given:

- the coupon of the underlying bond, and its price in the cash market;
- the interest rate for borrowing or lending funds, from the trade date to the maturity date of the futures contract. This is known as the *repo* rate.

For the purpose of deriving this pricing model we can ignore bid–offer spreads and borrowing and lending spreads. We set the following:

r is the repo rate;
rc is the bond's running yield;
P_{bond} is the price of the cash bond;
P_{fut} is the price of the futures contract;
t is the time to the expiry of the futures contract.

We can substitute these symbols into the cash flow profile for our earlier trade strategy, that of buying the bond and selling the future. This gives us:

Futures settlement cash flows

$$\text{Clean price for bond } = P_{fut}$$
$$\text{Bond accrued} = rc \times t \times P_{bond}$$
$$\text{Total proceeds } = P_{fut} + (rc \times t \times P_{bond})$$

Loan cash flows

Repayment of loan principal $= P_{bond}$

Loan interest $= r \times t \times P_{bond}$

Total outlay $= P_{bond} + (r \times t \times P_{bond})$

The profit from the trade would be the difference between the proceeds and outlay, which we can set as follows:

$$\text{Profit} = P_{fut} + rc \times t \times P_{bond} - P_{bond} + r \times t \times P_{bond} \quad (1.2)$$

We have seen how the futures price is at fair value when there is no profit to be gained from carrying out this trade, so if we set profit at 0, we obtain the following:

$$0 = P_{fut} + rc \times t \times P_{bond} - P_{bond} + r \times t \times P_{bond}$$

Solving this expression for the futures price P_{fut} gives us:

$$P_{fut} = P_{bond} + P_{bond}t(r - rc)$$

Rearranging this we get:

$$P_{fut} = P_{bond}(1 + t(r - rc)) \quad (1.3)$$

If we repeat the procedure for the other strategy, that of selling the bond and simultaneously buying the future, and set the profit to 0, we will obtain the same equation for the futures price as given in equation (1.3).

It is the level of the repo rate in the market, compared to the running yield on the underlying bond, that sets the price for the futures contract. From the examples used at the start of this section we can see that it is the cost of funding compared to the repo rate that determines if the trade strategy results in a profit. The $(r - rc)$ part of equation (1.3) is the net financing cost in the arbitrage trade, and is known as the *cost of carry*. If the running yield on the bond is higher than the funding cost (the repo rate) this is positive funding or *positive carry*. Negative funding (*negative carry*) is when the repo rate is higher than the running yield. The level of $(r - rc)$ will determine whether the futures price is trading above the cash market price or below it. If we have positive carry (when $rc > r$) then the futures price will trade below the cash market price, known as trading at a discount. Where $r > rc$ and we have negative carry then the futures price will be at a premium over the cash market price. If the net funding cost was 0, such that we had neither positive nor negative carry, then the futures price would be equal to the underlying bond price.

The cost of carry related to a bond futures contract is a function of the yield curve. In a positive yield curve environment the 3-month repo rate is likely to be lower than the running yield on a bond so that the cost of carry is likely to be positive. As there is generally only a liquid market in long bond futures out to contracts that mature up to 1 year from the trade date, with a positive yield curve it would be unusual to have a short-term repo rate higher than the running yield on the long bond. So, in such an environment we would have the future trading at a discount to the underlying cash bond. If there is a negative sloping yield curve the futures price will trade at a premium to the cash price. It is in circumstances of changes in the shape of the yield curve that opportunities for relative value and arbitrage trading arise, especially as the bond that is cheapest-to-deliver for the futures contract may change with large changes in the curve. A trading strategy that involved simultaneous and opposite positions in the cheapest-to-deliver (*CTD*) bond and the futures contract is what we have termed *cash-and-carry trading* or *basis trading*. However, by the law of no-arbitrage pricing, the payoff from such a trading strategy should be 0. If we set the profit from such a trading strategy as 0, we can obtain a pricing formula for the fair value of a futures contract, which summarises the discussion above, and states that the fair value futures price is a function of the cost of carry on the underlying bond. This is given as equation (1.4):

$$P_{fut} = \frac{(P_{bond} + AI_0) \times (1 + rt) - \sum_{i=1}^{N} C_i(1 + rt_{i,del}) - AI_{del}}{CF} \qquad (1.4)$$

AI_0 is the accrued interest on the underlying bond today;

AI_{del} is the accrued interest on the underlying bond on the expiry or delivery date (assuming the bond is delivered on the final day, which will be the case if the running yield on the bond is above the money market rate);

C_i is the ith coupon;

N is the number of coupons paid from today to the expiry or delivery date;

r is the repo rate;

t is the time period (in years) over which the trade takes place;

CF is the bond conversion factor;

$t_{i,del}$ is the period from receipt of the ith coupon to delivery.

1.3 HEDGING USING BOND FUTURES

We move on now to the concept of hedging bond positions using futures, essential prerequisite knowledge before tackling basis trading.

1.3.1 Introduction

Bond futures are used for a variety of purposes. Much of a day's trading in futures will be speculative; that is, a punt on the direction of the market. Another main use of futures is to hedge bond positions. In theory, when hedging a cash bond position with a bond futures contract, if cash and futures prices move together, then any loss from one position will be offset by a gain from the other. When prices move exactly in lock-step with each other, the hedge is considered perfect. In practice, the price of even the cheapest-to-deliver (CTD) bond (which one can view as being the bond being traded – implicitly – when one is trading the bond future) and the bond future will not move exactly in line with each other over a period of time. The difference between the cash price and the futures price is the *basis*. The risk that the basis will change in an unpredictable way is known as *basis risk*. Futures are a liquid and straightforward way of hedging a bond position. By hedging a bond position the trader or fund manager is hoping to balance the loss on the cash position by the profit gained from the hedge. However, the hedge will not be exact for all bonds except the CTD bond, which we can assume is the futures contract underlying bond. The basis risk in a hedge position arises because the bond being hedged is not identical to the CTD bond. The basic principle is that if the trader is long (or net long, where the desk is running long and short positions in different bonds) in the cash market, an equivalent number of futures contracts will be sold to set up the hedge. If the cash position is short the trader will buy futures. The hedging requirement can arise for different reasons. A market maker will wish to hedge positions arising out of client business, when they are unsure when the resulting bond positions will be unwound. A fund manager may, for example, know that they need to realise a cash sum at a specific time in the future to meet fund liabilities, and sell bonds at that time. The market maker will want to hedge against a drop in value of positions during the time the bonds are held. The fund manager will want to hedge against a rise in interest rates between now and the bond sale date, to protect the value of the portfolio.

When putting on the hedge position the key is to trade the correct number of futures contracts. This is determined by using the *hedge ratio* of the bond and the future, which is a function of the volatilities of the two instruments. The number of contracts to trade is calculated using the hedge ratio, which is given by:

$$\text{Hedge ratio} = \frac{\text{Volatility of bond to be hedged}}{\text{Volatility of hedging instrument}}.$$

Therefore, one needs to use the volatility values of each instrument. We can see from the calculation that if the bond is more volatile than the hedging instrument, then a greater amount of the hedging instrument will be required. Let us now look in greater detail at the hedge ratio.

There are different methods available to calculate hedge ratios. The most common ones are the conversion factor method, which can be used for deliverable bonds (also known as the *price factor* method) and the modified duration method (also known as the *basis point value* method).

Where a hedge is put on against a bond that is in the futures delivery basket it is common for the conversion factor to be used to calculate the hedge ratio. A conversion factor hedge ratio is more useful as it is transparent and remains constant, irrespective of any changes in the price of the cash bond or the futures contract. The number of futures contracts required to hedge a deliverable bond using the conversion factor hedge ratio is determined using equation (1.5):

$$\text{Number of contracts} = \frac{M_{bond} \times CF}{M_{fut}} \qquad (1.5)$$

where M is the nominal value of the bond or futures contract.

The conversion factor method may only be used for bonds in the delivery basket. It is important to ensure that this method is only used for these bonds. It is an erroneous procedure to use the ratio of conversion factors of two different bonds when calculating a hedge ratio, as detailed in Kolb (2000) and elsewhere.

Unlike the conversion factor method, the modified duration hedge ratio may be used for all bonds, both deliverable and non-deliverable. In calculating this hedge ratio the modified duration is multiplied by the dirty price of the cash bond to obtain the *basis point value* (*BPV*). The BPV represents the actual impact of a change in the yield on the price of a specific bond. The BPV allows the trader to calculate the hedge ratio to reflect the different price sensitivity of the chosen bond (compared to the CTD bond) to interest rate movements. The hedge ratio calculated using BPVs must be constantly updated, because it will change if the price of the bond and/or the futures contract changes. This may necessitate periodic adjustments to the number of lots used in the hedge. The number of futures contracts required to hedge a bond using the BPV method is calculated using the following:

$$\text{Number of contracts} = \frac{M_{bond}}{M_{fut}} \times \frac{BPV_{bond}}{BPV_{fut}} \qquad (1.6)$$

where the BPV of a futures contract is defined with respect to the BPV of its CTD bond, as given by equation (1.7):

$$BPV_{fut} = \frac{BPV_{CTDbond}}{CF_{CTDbond}} \qquad (1.7)$$

The simplest hedge procedure to undertake is one for a position consisting of only one bond, the CTD bond. The relationship between the futures price and the price of the CTD given by equation (1.4) indicates that the price of the future will move for moves in the price of the CTD bond, so therefore we may set:

$$\Delta P_{fut} \cong \frac{\Delta P_{Bond}}{CF} \qquad (1.8)$$

where *CF* is the CTD conversion factor.

The price of the futures contract, over time, does not move tick-for-tick with the CTD bond (although it may on an intra-day basis) but rather by the amount of the change divided by the conversion factor. It is apparent, therefore, that to hedge a position in the CTD bond we must hold the number of futures contracts equivalent to the value of bonds held multiplied by the conversion factor. Obviously, if a conversion factor is less than 1, the number of futures contracts will be less than the equivalent nominal value of the cash position; the opposite is true for bonds that have a conversion factor greater than 1. However, the hedge is not as simple as dividing the nominal value of the bond position by the nominal value represented by one futures contract.

To measure the effectiveness of the hedge position, it is necessary to compare the performance of the futures position with that of the cash bond position, and to see how much the hedge instrument mirrored the performance of the cash instrument. A simple calculation is made to measure the effectiveness of the hedge, given by equation (1.9), which is the percentage value of the hedge effectiveness:

$$\text{Hedge effectiveness} = -\left(\frac{\text{Fut } p/l}{\text{Bond } p/l}\right) \times 100 \quad (1.9)$$

where $p/l = \text{Profit and loss}$.

1.3.2 Hedging a bond portfolio

The principles established above may be applied when hedging a portfolio containing a number of bonds. It is more realistic to consider a portfolio holding not just bonds that are outside the delivery basket, but are also not government bonds. In this case we need to calculate the number of futures contracts to put on as a hedge based on the volatility of each bond in the portfolio compared to the volatility of the CTD bond. Note that, in practice, there is usually more than one futures contract that may be used as the hedge instrument. For example, in the sterling market it would be more sensible to use LIFFE's medium gilt contract, whose underlying bond has a notional maturity of 4–7 years, if hedging a portfolio of short- to medium-dated bonds. However, for the purposes of illustration we will assume that only one contract, the long bond, is available. To calculate the number of futures contracts required to hold as a hedge against any specific bond, we use equation (1.10):

$$\text{Hedge} = \frac{M_{bond}}{M_{fut}} \times Vol_{bond/CTD} \times Vol_{CTD/fut} \quad (1.10)$$

where $\quad M =$ Nominal value of the bond or future;

$Vol_{bond/CTD} =$ Relative volatility of the bond being hedged compared to that of the CTD bond;

$Vol_{CTD/fut} =$ Relative volatility of the CTD bond compared to that of the future.

It is not necessarily straightforward to determine the relative volatility of a bond vis-à-vis the CTD bond. If the bond being hedged is a government bond, we can calculate the relative volatility using the two bonds' modified duration. This is because the yields of both may be safely assumed to be strongly positively correlated. If, however, the bond being hedged is a corporate bond and/or non-vanilla bond, we must obtain the relative volatility using regression analysis, as the yields between the two bonds may not be strongly positively correlated. This is apparent when one remembers that the yield spread of corporate bonds over government bonds is not constant, and will fluctuate with changes in government bond yields and corporate credit risk. To use regression analysis to determine relative volatilities, historical price data on the bond is required; the daily price moves in the target bond and the CTD bond are then analysed to assess the slope of the regression line. In this section we will restrict the discussion to a portfolio of government bonds. If we are hedging a portfolio of government bonds we can use equation (1.11) to determine relative volatility values, based on the modified duration of each of the bonds in the portfolio:

$$Vol_{bond/CTD} = \frac{\Delta P_{bond}}{\Delta P_{CTD}} = \frac{MD_{bond} \times P_{bond}}{MD_{CTD} \times P_{CTD}} \quad (1.11)$$

where MD is the modified duration of the bond being hedged or the CTD bond, as appropriate.[1] Once we have calculated the relative volatility of the bond being hedged, equation (1.12) – obtained from (1.8) and (1.11) – tells us that the relative volatility of the CTD bond to that of the futures contract is approximately the same as its conversion factor. We are then in a position to calculate the futures hedge for each bond in a portfolio:

$$Vol_{CTD/fut} = \frac{\Delta P_{CTD}}{\Delta P_{fut}} \approx CF_{CTD} \quad (1.12)$$

Table 1.4 shows a portfolio of five UK gilts on 20 October 1999. The nominal value of the bonds in the portfolio is £200 million, and the bonds have a market

---

[1] In certain textbooks and practitioner research documents, it is suggested that the ratio of the conversion factors of the bond being hedged (if it is in the delivery basket) and the CTD bond can be used to determine the relative volatility of the target bond. This is a specious argument. The conversion factor of a deliverable bond is the price factor that will set the yield of the bond equal to the notional coupon of the futures contract on the delivery date, and it is a function mainly of the coupon of the deliverable bond. The price volatility of a bond, on the other hand, is a measure of its modified duration, which is a function of the bond's duration (that is, the weighted average term to maturity). Therefore, using conversion factors to measure volatility levels will produce erroneous results. It is important not to misuse conversion factors when arranging hedge ratios.

Table 1.4 Bond futures hedge for hypothetical gilt portfolio, 20 October 1999

CTD	5.75% 2009				Modified duration 7.234 565 567		
Conversion factor 0.912 495 0				Price 99.84			
Bond	Nominal amount	Price (£m)	Yield (%)	Duration	Modified duration	Relative volatility	Number of contracts
UKT 8% 2000	12	102.17	5.972	1.072	1.011 587 967	0.143 090 242	15.67
UKT 7% 2002	5	101.50	6.367	2.388	2.245 057 208	0.315 483 336	14.39
UKT 5% 2004	38	94.74	6.327	4.104	3.859 791 022	0.506 267 61	175.55
UKT 5.75% 2009	100	99.84	5.770	7.652	7.234 565 567	1.00	912.50
UKT 6% 2028	45	119.25	4.770	15.031	14.346 664 12	2.368 603 078	972.60
Total	200						2090.71

value excluding accrued interest of £206.84 million. Only one of the bonds is a deliverable bond, the $5\frac{3}{4}\%$ 2009 gilt which is in fact the CTD bond. For the Dec99 futures contract the bond had a conversion factor of 0.912 495 0. The fact that this bond is the CTD explains why it has a relative volatility of 1. We calculate the number of futures contracts required to hedge each position, using the equations listed above. For example, the hedge requirement for the position in the 7% 2002 gilt was calculated as follows:

$$\frac{5,000,000}{100,000} \times \frac{2.245 \times 101.50}{7.235 \times 99.84} \times 0.912\,495\,0 = 14.39$$

The volatility of all the bonds is calculated relative to the CTD bond, and the number of futures contracts determined using the conversion factor for the CTD bond. The bond with the highest volatility is not surprisingly the 6% 2028, which has the longest maturity of all the bonds and hence the highest modified duration.

We note from Table 1.4 that the portfolio requires a hedge position of 2091 futures contracts. This illustrates how a 'rough-and-ready' estimate of the hedging requirement, based on nominal values, would be insufficient as that would suggest a hedge position of only 2000 contracts.

The effectiveness of the hedge must be monitored over time. No hedge will be completely perfect, however, and the calculation illustrated above, as it uses modified duration value, does not take into account the convexity effect of the bonds. The reason why a futures hedge will not be perfect is because, in practice, the price of the futures contract will not move tick-for-tick with the CTD bond, at least not over a period of time. This is the basis risk that is inherent in hedging cash bonds with futures. In addition, the calculation of the hedge is only completely accurate for a parallel shift in yields, as it is based on modified duration; so, as the yield curve changes around pivots, the hedge will move out of line. Finally, the long gilt future is not the appropriate contract to use to hedge three of the bonds in the portfolio, or over 25% of the portfolio by nominal value. This is because these bonds are short- or medium-dated, and so their price movements will not track the futures price as closely as longer-dated bonds. In this case, the more appropriate futures contract to use would have been the medium gilt contract, or (for the first bond, the 8% 2000) a strip of short sterling contracts. Using shorter dated instruments would reduce some of the basis risk contained in the portfolio hedge.

1.3.3   The margin process

Institutions buying and selling futures on an exchange deal with only one counterparty at all times, the exchange clearing house. The clearing house is responsible for the settlement of all contracts, including managing the delivery process. A central clearing mechanism eliminates counterparty risk for anyone dealing on the exchange, because the clearing house guarantees the settlement of all transactions. The clearing house may be owned by the exchange itself, such as the one associated with the Chicago Mercantile Exchange (the *CME*

Clearinghouse) or it may be a separate entity, such as the LCH, which settles transactions on LIFFE. The LCH is also involved in running clearing systems for swaps and repo products in certain currencies. One of the key benefits to the market of the clearing house mechanism is that counterparty risk, as it is transferred to the clearing house, is virtually eliminated. The mechanism that enables the clearing house to accept the counterparty risk is the *margin* process that is employed at all futures exchanges. A bank or local trader must deposit margin before commencing dealing on the exchange; each day a further amount must be deposited or will be returned, depending on the results of the day's trading activity.

The exchange will specify the level of margin that must be deposited for each type of futures contract that a bank wishes to deal in. The *initial margin* will be a fixed sum per lot; so, for example, if the margin was £1,000 per lot an opening position of 100 lots would require margin of £100,000. Once initial margin has been deposited, there is a mark-to-market of all positions at the close of business; exchange-traded instruments are the most transparent products in the market, and the closing price is not only known to everyone, it is also indisputable. The closing price is also known as the *settlement price*. Any losses suffered by a trading counterparty, whether closed out or run overnight, are entered as a debit on the party's account and must be paid the next day. Trading profits are credited and may be withdrawn from the margin account the next day. This daily process is known as *variation margining*. Thus, the margin account is updated on a daily basis and the maximum loss that must be made up on any morning is the maximum price movement that occurred the previous day. It is a serious issue if a trading party is unable to meet a margin call. In such a case, the exchange will order it to cease trading, and will also liquidate all its open positions; any losses will be met out of the firm's margin account. If the level of funds in the margin account is insufficient, the losses will be made good from funds paid out of a general fund run by the clearing house, which is maintained by all members of the exchange.

Payment of margin is made by electronic funds transfer between the trading party's bank account and the clearing house. Initial margin is usually paid in cash, although clearing houses will also accept high-quality securities such as T-bills or certain government bonds, to the value of the margin required. Variation margin is always cash. The advantage of depositing securities rather than cash is that the depositing firm earns interest on its margin. This is not available on a cash margin, and the interest foregone on a cash margin is effectively the cost of trading futures on the exchange. However, if securities are used, there is effectively no cost associated with trading on the exchange (we ignore, of course, infrastructure costs and staff salaries).

The daily settlement of exchange-traded futures contracts, as opposed to when the contract expires or the position is closed out, is the main reason why futures prices are not equal to forward prices for long-dated instruments.

Appendix 1.A CONVERSION FACTOR FOR THE LONG GILT FUTURE

Here we describe the process used for the calculation of the *conversion factor* or *price factor* for deliverable bonds of the long gilt contract. The contract specifies a bond of maturity $8\frac{3}{4}$ 13 years and a notional coupon of 7%.[2] For each bond that is eligible to be in the delivery basket, the conversion factor is given by the following equation: $P(7)/100$ where the numerator $P(7)$ is equal to the price per £100 nominal of the deliverable gilt at which it has a gross redemption yield of 7%, calculated as at the 1st day of the delivery month, less the accrued interest on the bond on that day. This calculation uses the formulae given in equation (1.13) and the equation used to calculate accrued interest. The numerator $P(7)$ is given by equation (1.13):

$$p(7) = \frac{1}{1.035^{t/s}} \left(c_1 + \frac{c_2}{1.035} + \frac{C}{0.07} \left(\frac{1}{1.035} - \frac{1}{1.035^n} \right) \right.$$
$$\left. + \frac{100}{1.035^n} \right) - AI \qquad (1.13)$$

where c_1 = Cash flow due on the following quasi-coupon date, per £100 nominal of the gilt. c_1 will be 0 if the 1st day of the delivery month occurs in the ex-dividend period or if the gilt has a long first

---

[2] The notional coupon was changed from 7% to 6% from the Mar04 contract onwards.

coupon period and the 1st day of the delivery month occurs in the first full coupon period. c_1 will be less than c_2 if the 1st day of the delivery month falls in a short first coupon period. c_1 will be greater than c_2 if the 1st day of the delivery month falls in a long first coupon period and the 1st day of the delivery month occurs in the second full coupon period;

$c_2 =$ Cash flow due on the next but one quasi-coupon date, per £100 nominal of the gilt. c_1 will be greater than c_2 if the 1st day of the delivery month falls in a long first coupon period and in the first full coupon period. In all other cases, $c_2 = C/2$; C is the annual coupon of the gilt, per £100 nominal;

$t =$ Number of calendar days from and including the 1st day of the delivery month up to but excluding the next quasi-coupon date;

$s =$ Number of calendar days in the full coupon period in which the first day of the delivery month occurs;

$n =$ Number of full coupon periods between the following quasi-coupon date and the redemption date;

$AI =$ Accrued interest per £100 nominal of the gilt.

The accrued interest used in equation (1.13) is given according to the following procedures.

If the 1st day of the delivery month occurs in a standard coupon period, and the 1st day of the delivery month occurs on or before the ex-dividend date, then:

$$AI = \frac{t}{s} \times \frac{C}{2} \qquad (1.14)$$

If the 1st day of the delivery month occurs in a standard coupon period, and the 1st day of the delivery month occurs after the ex-dividend date, then:

$$AI = \left(\frac{t}{s} - 1\right) \times \frac{C}{2} \qquad (1.15)$$

where $t =$ Number of calendar days from and including the last coupon date up to but excluding the 1st day of the delivery month;

           $s =$ Number of calendar days in the full coupon period in which the 1st day of the delivery month occurs.

If the 1st day of the delivery month occurs in a short first coupon period, and the 1st day of the delivery month occurs on or before the ex-dividend date, then:

$$AI = \frac{t^*}{s} \times \frac{C}{2} \qquad (1.16)$$

If the 1st day of the delivery month occurs in a short first coupon period, and the 1st day of the delivery month occurs after the ex-dividend date, then:

$$AI = \frac{t^* - n}{s} \times \frac{C}{2} \qquad (1.17)$$

where $t =$ Number of calendar days from and including the issue date up to but excluding the 1st day of the delivery month;

$n =$ Number of calendar days from and including the issue date up to but excluding the next quasi-coupon date.

If the 1st day of the delivery month occurs in a long first coupon period, and during the first full coupon period, then:

$$AI = \frac{u}{s_1} \times \frac{C}{2} \qquad (1.18)$$

If the 1st day of the delivery month occurs in a long first coupon period, and during the second full coupon period and on or before the ex-dividend date, then:

$$AI = \left(\frac{p_1}{s_1} + \frac{p_2}{s_2} \right) \times \frac{C}{2} \qquad (1.19)$$

If the 1st day of the delivery month occurs in a long first coupon period, and during the second full coupon period and after the ex-dividend date, then:

$$AI = \left(\frac{p_2}{s_2} - 1 \right) \times \frac{C}{2} \qquad (1.20)$$

where $u =$ Number of calendar days from and including the issue date up to but excluding the 1st day of the delivery month;

$s_1 =$ Number of calendar days in the full coupon period in which the issue date occurs;

$s_2 =$ Number of days in the next full coupon period after the full coupon period in which the issue date occurs;

$p_1 =$ Number of calendar days from and including the issue date up to but excluding the next quasi-coupon date;

$p_2 =$ Number of calendar days from and including the quasi-coupon date after the issue date up to but excluding the 1st day of the delivery month which falls in the next full coupon period after the full coupon period in which the issue date occurs.

SELECTED BIBLIOGRAPHY

Burghardt, G. (1994) *The Treasury Bond Basis*. McGraw-Hill.

Fabozzi, F. (1993) *Fixed Income Mathematics*. Probus.

Kolb, R. (2000) *Futures, Options and Swaps*. Blackwell.

Chapter

2

....

THE GOVERNMENT
BOND BASIS

B asis trading, also known as *cash and carry* trading, refers to the activity of simultaneously trading cash bonds and the related bond futures contract. The *basis* is the difference between the price of a cash market asset (in this book we consider only bonds as the underlying asset) and its price as implied in the futures markets. An open repo market is essential for the smooth operation of basis trading. Most futures exchanges offer at least one bond futures contract. Major exchanges such as the Chicago Board of Trade (*CBOT*) offer contracts along the entire yield curve; others such as the London International Financial Futures Exchange (*LIFFE*) provide a market in contracts on bonds denominated in a range of major currencies.

So, the *basis* of a futures contract is the difference between the spot price of an asset and its price for future delivery as implied by the price of a futures contract written on the asset. Futures contracts are exchange-traded standardised instruments, so they are a form of what is termed a *forward* instrument, a contract that describes the forward delivery of an asset at a price agreed today. The pricing of forwards and futures follows similar principles but, as we shall see, contains significant detail differences between the two. The simultaneous trading of futures contracts written on government bonds and the bonds themselves is an important part of the government repo markets; in this, and the two subsequent chapters (Chapters 3 and 4), we review the essential elements of this type of trading.

We begin with basic concepts of forward pricing, before looking at the determinants of the basis, hedging using bond futures, trading the basis and an introduction to trading strategy. We also look at the concept of the *cheapest-to-deliver* (*CTD*) bond, and the two ways in which this is measured: the net basis and the *implied repo rate*. As ever, readers are directed to the bibliography, particularly the book by Burghardt *et al.* (1994), which is an excellent reference work. It reads very accessibly and contains insights useful for all bond market participants.

We begin with the concepts of forward and futures pricing, and futures contracts. This is essential background enabling us to discuss the implied repo rate and basis trading in Chapter 3. The repo desk plays a crucial role in basis trading and, just like forward pricing principles, an appreciation of the repo function is also key to understanding the bond basis. First, we discuss some basic concepts in futures pricing and then look at the concept of the bond basis.

2.1   AN INTRODUCTION TO FORWARD PRICING

2.1.1   Introduction

Let's first look at a qualitative way of considering the forward bond basis, connected with the coupon and running cost on cash bonds. This approach reads more accessibly for those who wish a more specific application to forward pricing on bond assets.

An investor assessing whether an asset is worth purchasing spot or forward must consider two issues: whether there is an income stream associated with the asset, in which case this would be foregone if the asset was purchased forward; and if there are any holding costs associated with the asset if it is purchased spot. The forward price on a bond must reflect these same considerations, so a buyer will consider the effect of income foregone and *carry* costs and assess the relative gain of spot versus forward purchase. In real terms then, we are comparing the income stream of the bond coupon against the interest rate on funds borrowed to purchase the bond.[1]

An investor who is long a cash bond will receive coupon income, and this is accrued on a daily basis. This is purely an accounting convention and has no bearing on the current interest rate or the current price of the bond.[2] An investor who purchases a bond forward is foregoing the income during the time to delivery, and this factor should presumably be incorporated into the forward price. What of the funding (carry) cost involved? This can be calculated from the current money market rate provided the term of the funding is known with

---

[1] We assume a leveraged investor: if spot purchase is desired, the investor will borrow the funds used to buy the bond.

[2] Van Deventer (1997) states that the accrued interest concept is 'an arbitrary calculation that has no economic meaning.' This is because it reflects the coupon and not current interest rates; so, in other words, it reflects interest rates at the time of issue. The coupon accrued is identical whatever current interest rates may be. It's worth purchasing this book as it contains accessible accounts of a number of fixed income analytic techniques.

certainty. So, if we now consider a 3-month forward contract on a bond against the current spot price of the same bond, the investor must assess:

- the coupon income that would be received during the 3-month period;
- the interest charge on funds borrowed during the 3-month period.

Let us say that the difference between these two values was exactly 1.00. For the forward contract to be a worthwhile purchase, it would have to be at least 1.00 lower in price than the spot price. This is known as the forward discount. Otherwise the investor is better off buying the bond for spot delivery. However, if the price is much lower than 1.00, investors will only buy forward (while cash bond holders would sell their holdings and repurchase forward). This would force the forward price back into line to its *fair value*. The forward price discount is known as the *basis*. The basis exists in all markets where there is a choice available between spot and forward delivery, and not just in financial derivatives. For bonds the basis can be assessed by reference to the current price of the underlying asset, the income stream (coupon), the time to maturity of the forward contract and the current level of interest rates.

2.1.2 Illustrating the forward bond basis

Now, let us look at an illustration, using the September 2000 long gilt contract. We use the coupon income from the cheapest-to-deliver (*CTD*) bond, the 5.75% 2009 gilt. We haven't discussed the concept of the CTD yet;

however, ignore the CTD element for now, and assume
a constant money market borrowing rate (the repo rate)
during the 3 months of the futures contract from 29 June
2000 to 27 September 2000.

Intuitively, we would expect the basis to move towards
0, as the contract approached maturity. After all, what is
the price of something for delivery now if not the spot
price? First, we consider the yield of the bond against the
yield of the futures contract. This is illustrated in Figure
2.1. There is slight convergence towards the end; however, if we plot the basis itself, this does converge to 0 as
expected. This is shown in Figure 2.2. As the contract
approaches maturity, the basis becomes more and more
sensitive to slight changes in bond price or financing
rates, hence the exaggerated spike. For instance, if short-
term repo rates decrease, while the coupon income on
the bond remains unchanged, an investor would be faced
with a lower level of foregone return as a result of lower
financing costs. This makes it more attractive for an
investor to buy the bond for spot delivery, and so the

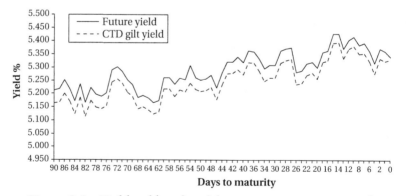

Figure 2.1   Yields of bond and futures contract compared.
Source: LIFFE and Bloomberg.

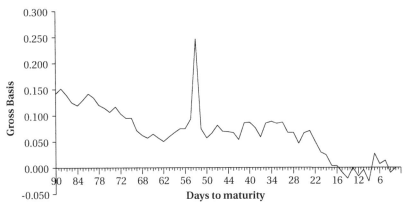

Figure 2.2   Convergence of basis towards 0.
Source: LIFFE and Bloomberg.

basis will rise as demand for the forward (or future, to be precise) declines.

Essentially, when the repo rate is significantly below the bond yield,[3] the basis will be high. If the repo rate then rises the basis will fall, and this indicates the smaller interest-rate differential between the repo rate and the bond yield. If the repo rate rises to a point where it is above the bond yield, the basis will turn negative. In fact, this occurred briefly during the later stages of the life of the September 2000 gilt future as shown above. A negative basis indicates that the price for forward delivery exceeds that for spot delivery.

To reiterate then, the forward basis quantifies the relationship between the income generated by the underlying asset and the costs incurred by owning it.[4] As we are

---

[3] The bond's running yield, or flat yield, is usually used.
[4] Readers are invited to think of assets for which the forward basis is routinely negative ...

concerned with bond futures specifically, the basis will reflect the relationship between the underlying bond's coupon stream and the repo financing rate if holding the bond. Forward contracts for bonds exhibit the basis. Futures contracts, which are standardised forward contracts traded on an organised exchange, are priced on the same principles as forwards and, so therefore, also exhibit the basis. Section 2.2 considers forward pricing in a more formal way.

2.2 FORWARDS AND FUTURES VALUATION

Let us now take a more rigorous look at forward valuation. To begin our discussion of derivative instruments, we discuss the valuation and analysis of forward and futures contracts; here, we develop basic valuation concepts. The discussion follows, with permission, the approach described in Rubinstein (1999), as shown in section 2.2 of that text.[5]

2.2.1 Introduction

A forward contract is an agreement between two parties in which the buyer contracts to purchase from the seller a specified asset, for delivery at a future date, at a price agreed today. The terms are set so that the present value

---

[5] This is a very good book and highly recommended, and for all students and practitioners interested in capital markets, not just those involved with derivative instruments.

of the contract is 0. For the forthcoming analysis we use the following notation:

P = Current price of the underlying asset, also known as the *spot* price;

P_T = Price of the underlying asset at the time of delivery;

X = Delivery price of the forward contract;

T = Term to maturity of the contract in years, also referred to as the time-to-delivery;

r = Risk-free interest rate;

R = Return of the payout or its *yield*;

F = Current price of the forward contract.

The payoff of a forward contract is therefore given by:

$$P_T - X \qquad (2.1)$$

with X set at the start so that the present value of $(P_T - X)$ is 0. The payout yield is calculated by obtaining the percentage of the spot price that is paid out on expiry.

2.2.2 Forwards

When a forward contract is written, its delivery price is set so that the present value of the payout is 0. This means that the forward price F is then the price on delivery which would make the present value of the payout, on the delivery date, equal to 0. That is, at the start $F = X$. This is the case only on day 1 of the contract, however. From then until the contract expiry the value of X is fixed, but the forward price F will fluctuate continuously until delivery. It is the behaviour of this forward price that we wish to examine. For instance, generally as the spot price of the underlying increases, so the price of a forward contract written on the asset also increases; and *vice versa*. At this stage, it is important to remember that the forward price of a contract is not the same as the value of the contract, and the terms of the agreement are set so that at inception the value is 0. The relationship given above is used to show that an equation can be derived which relates F to P, T, r and R.

Consider first the profit/loss profile for a forward contract. This is shown in Figure 2.3. The price of the forward can be shown to be related to the underlying variables as:

$$F = S\left(\frac{r}{R}\right)^T \qquad (2.2)$$

and for the 1-year contract highlighted in Figure 2.3 is 52.5, where the parameters are $S = 50$, $r = 1.05$ and $R = 1.00$.

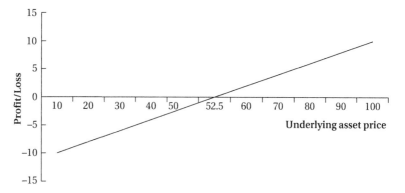

Figure 2.3   Forward contract profit/loss profile.

2.2.3 Futures

Forward contracts are tailor-made instruments designed to meet specific individual requirements. *Futures* contracts, on the other hand, are standardised contracts that are traded on recognised futures exchanges. Apart from this, the significant difference between them, and the feature that influences differences between forward and futures prices, is that profits or losses that are gained or suffered in futures trading are paid out at the end of the day. This does not occur with forwards. The majority of futures contracts positions are always closed out; that is, the position is netted out to 0 before the expiry of the contract. If a position is run into the delivery month, depending on the terms and conditions of the particular exchange, the party that is long future may be delivered into. Settlement is by physical delivery in the case of commodity futures or in cash in the case of certain financial futures. Bond futures are financial futures where any bond that is in the *delivery basket* for that contract will be delivered to the long future. With both physical and financial futures, only a very small percentage of contracts are actually delivered into as the majority of trading is undertaken for hedging and speculative purposes.

With futures contracts, as all previous trading profits and losses have been settled, on the day of expiry only the additional change from the previous day needs to be accounted for. With a forward contract all loss or gain is rolled up until the expiry day and handed over as a total amount on this day.[6]

2.2.4   Forwards and futures

Cash flow differences

We can now look at the cash flow treatment of the two contracts in greater detail. This is illustrated in Table 2.1, which uses F to denote the price of the futures contract as well. The table shows the payoff schedule at the end of each trading day for the two instruments; assume that they have identical terms. With the forward there is no cash flow on intermediate dates, whereas with the futures contract there is. As with the forward contract, the price of the future fixes the present value of the futures contract at 0. Each day the change in price, which at the end of the day is *marked-to-market* at the *close* price, will have resulted in either a profit or gain,[7] which is handed over or received each day as appropriate. The process of daily settlement of price movements means that the nominal delivery price can be reset each day so that the present value of the contract is always 0. This means that the future and nominal delivery prices of a futures contract are the same at the end of each trading day.

---

[6] We assume the parties have traded only one forward contract between them. If, as is more accurate to assume, a large number of contracts have been traded across a number of different maturity periods and perhaps instruments, as contracts expire only the net loss or gain is transferred between counterparties.

[7] Or no profit or gain if the closing price is unchanged from the previous day's closing price, a *doji* as technical traders call it.

Table 2.1 Cash flow process for forwards and futures contracts.

Time	Forward contract	Futures contract
0	0	0
1	0	$F_1 - F$
2	0	$F_2 - F_1$
3	0	$F_3 - F_2$
4	0	$F_4 - F_3$
5	0	$F_5 - F_4$
...	0	...
...	0	...
...	0	...
$T - 1$	0	$F_{T-1} - F_{T-2}$
T	$P_T - F$	$P_T - F_{T-1}$
Total	$P_T - F$	$P_T - F$

We see in Table 2.1 that there are no cash flows changing hands between counterparties to a forward contract. The price of a futures contract is reset each day; after day 1 this means it is reset from F to F_1. The amount $(F_1 - F)$, if positive, is handed over by the short future to the long future. If this amount is negative, it is paid by the long future to the short. On the expiry day T of the contract the long future will receive a settlement amount equal to $P_T - F_{T-1}$ which expresses the relationship between the price of the future and the price of the underlying asset. As significant, the daily cash flows transferred when holding a futures contract cancel each other out, so that on expiry the value of the contract is (at this stage) identical to that for a forward, that is $(P_T - F)$.

With exchange-traded contracts all market participants are deemed to conduct their trading with a central counterparty, the exchange's clearing house. This eliminates counterparty risk in all transactions, and the clearing house is able to guarantee each bargain because all participants are required to contribute to its clearing fund. This is by the process of *margin*, by which each participant deposits an *initial margin* and then, as its profits or losses are recorded, deposits further *variation margin* on a daily basis. The marking-to-market of futures contracts is an essential part of this margin process. A good description of the exchange clearing process is contained in Kolb (2000).

This is the key difference between future and forward contracts. If holding a futures position that is recording a daily profit, the receipt of this profit on a daily basis is advantageous because the funds can be reinvested while the position is still maintained. This is not available with a forward. Equally, losses are suffered on a daily basis that are not suffered by the holder of a loss-making forward position.

2.2.5 Relationship between forward and future price

Continuing with the analysis contained in Rubinstein (1999), we wish to illustrate that under certain specified assumptions, the price of futures and forwards written with identical terms must be the same.

This can be shown in the following way. Consider two trading strategies of identical term to maturity and written on the same underlying asset; one strategy uses forward contracts while the other uses futures. Both strategies require no initial investment and are *self-financing*. The assumptions are:

- the absence of risk-free arbitrage opportunities;
- the existence of an economist's perfect market;
- certainty of returns.

Under these conditions, it can be shown that the forward and future price must be identical. In this analysis the return r is the daily return (or instantaneous money market rate) and T is the maturity term in days. Let's look further at the strategies.

For the strategy employing forwards, we buy r^T forward contracts. The start forward price is $F = X$, but of course there is no cash outlay at the start, and the payoff on expiry is:

$$r^T(P_T - F)$$

The futures strategy is more involved, due to the daily margin cash flows that are received or paid during the term of the trade. On day 1 we buy r contracts each priced at F. After the close we receive $F_1 - F$. The position is closed out and the cash received is invested at the daily rate r up to the expiry date. The return on this cash is r^{T-1} which means that on expiry we will receive an amount of:

$$r(F_1 - F)r^{T-1}$$

The next day we purchase r^2 futures contracts at the price of F_1 and at the close the cash flow received of

$F_2 - F_1$ is invested at the close of trading at r^{T-2}. Again we will receive on expiry a sum equal to:

$$r^2(F_2 - F_1)r^{T-2}$$

This process is repeated until the expiry date, which we assume to be the delivery date. What is the net effect of following this strategy? We will receive on the expiry date a set of maturing cash flows that have been invested daily from the end of day 1. The cash sums will be:

$$r^T(F_1 - F) + r^T(F_2 - F_1) + r^T(F_3 - F_2) + \cdots + r^T(P_T - F_{T-1})$$

which nets to:

$$r^T(P_T - F)$$

which is also the payoff from the forward contract strategy. Both strategies have a zero cash outlay and are self-financing. The key point is that if indeed we are saying that:

$$r^T(P_T - F)_{forward} = r^T(P_T - F)_{future} \qquad (2.3)$$

for the assumption of no-arbitrage to hold, then $F_{forward} = F_{future}$.

2.2.6   The forward–spot parity

We can use the forward strategy to imply the forward price provided we know the current price of the underlying and the money market interest rate. A numerical example of the forward strategy is given at Figure 2.4, with the same parameters given earlier. We assume no-arbitrage and a perfect frictionless market.

	Cash flows	
	Start date	Expiry
Buy forward contract	0	$P_T - F$
Buy one unit of the underlying asset	-50	P_T
Borrow zero present-value of forward price	$F/1.05$	F
Total	$-50 + F/1.05$	$P_T - F$

Result
Set $-50 + F/1.05$ equal to 0
(no-arbitrage condition)
Therefore $F = 52.5$

Figure 2.4   Forward strategy.

What Figure 2.4 is saying is that it is possible to replicate the payoff profile we observed in Figure 2.3 by a portfolio composed of one unit of the underlying asset, the purchase of which is financed by borrowing a sum that is equal to the present value of the forward price. This borrowing is repaid on maturity and is equal to $(F/1.05) \times 1.05$ which is in fact F. In the absence of arbitrage opportunity the cost of forming the portfolio will be identical to that of the forward itself. However, we have set the current cost of the forward contract at 0, which gives us:

$$-50 + \frac{F}{1.05} = 0$$

We solve this expression to obtain F and this is 52.50.

The price of the forward contract is 52.50, although the present value of the forward contract when it is written is 0. Following Rubinstein, we prove this in Figure 2.5.

	Cash flows	
	Start date	Expiry
Buy forward contract	0	$P_T - F$
Buy R^{-T} units of the underlying asset	$-PR^{-T}$	P_T
Borrow zero present-value of forward price	Fr^{-T}	$-F$
Total	$-PR^{-T} + Fr^{-T}$	$P_T - F$

Result

Set $-PR^{-T} + Fr^{-T} = 0$

Therefore, $F = P(r/R)^T$

Figure 2.5   Algebraic proof of forward price.

What Figure 2.5 states is that the payoff profile for the forward can be replicated precisely by setting up a portfolio that holds R^{-T} units of the underlying asset, which is funded through borrowing a sum equal to the present value of the forward price. This borrowing is repaid at maturity, this amount being equal to:

$$(Fr^{-T})r^T = F$$

The portfolio has an identical payoff profile (by design) to the forward, this being $(P_T - F)$. In a no-arbitrage environment, the cost of setting up the portfolio must be equal to the current price of the forward, as they have identical payoffs and if one was cheaper than the other, there would be a risk-free profit for a trader who bought the cheap instrument and shorted the dear one. However, we set the current cost of the forward (its present value)

at 0, which means the cost of constructing the duplicat-
ing portfolio must therefore be 0 as well. This gives us:

$$-PR^{-T} + Fr^{-T} = 0$$

which allows us to solve for the forward price F.

The significant aspect for the buyer of a forward contract
is that the payoff of the forward is identical to that of a
portfolio containing an equivalent amount of the underlying asset, which has been constructed using borrowed
funds. The portfolio is known as the *replicating portfolio*. The price of the forward contract is a function of
the current underlying spot price, the risk-free or money
market interest rate, the payoff and the maturity of the
contract. To recap then, the forward–spot parity states
that:

$$F = P\left(\frac{r}{R}\right)^{T} \tag{2.4}$$

It can be shown that neither of the possibilities
$F > P(r/R)^{T}$ or $F < P(r/R)^{T}$ will hold unless arbitrage
possibilities are admitted. The only possibility is (2.4),
at which the futures price is *fair value.*

2.2.7 The basis and implied repo rate

For later analysis, we introduce now some terms used in
the futures markets.

The difference between the price of a futures contract
and the current underlying spot price is known as the
basis. For bond futures contracts, which are written not

on a specific bond but a *notional* bond that can in fact be represented by any bond that fits within the contract terms, the size of the basis is given by (2.5):

$$Basis = P_{bond} - (P_{fut} \times CF) \qquad (2.5)$$

where the basis is the *gross basis* and *CF* is the *conversion factor* for the bond in question. All delivery-eligible bonds are said to be in the *delivery basket*. The conversion factor equalizes each deliverable bond to the futures price.[8] The size of the gross basis represents the cost of carry associated with the bond from today to the delivery date. The bond with the lowest basis associated with it is known as the *cheapest-to-deliver* bond. The magnitude of the basis changes continuously and this uncertainty is termed *basis risk*. Generally, the basis declines over time as the maturity of the contract approaches, and converges to 0 on the expiry date. The significance of basis risk is greatest for market participants who use futures contracts for hedging positions held in the underlying asset. The basis is positive or negative according to the type of market in question, and is a function of issues such as *cost of carry*. When the basis is positive, that is $F > P$, the situation is described as a *contango*, and is common in precious metals markets. A negative basis $P < F$ is described as *backwardation* and is common in oil contracts and foreign currency markets.

---

[8] For a description and analysis of bond futures contracts, the basis, implied repo and the cheapest-to-deliver bond, see Burghardt *et al.* (1994), an excellent account of the analysis of the Treasury bond basis. Plona (1997) is also a readable treatment of the European government bond basis.

The hedging of futures and the underlying asset requires a keen observation of the basis. To hedge a position in a futures contract, one could run an opposite position in the underlying. However, running such a position incurs the cost of carry referred to above, which, depending on the nature of the asset, may include storage costs, opportunity cost of interest foregone, funding costs of holding the asset and so on. The futures price may be analysed in terms of the forward–spot parity relationship and the risk-free interest rate. If we say that the risk-free rate is:

$$r - 1$$

and the forward–spot parity is:

$$F = P\left(\frac{r}{R}\right)^T$$

we can set:

$$r - 1 = R\left(\frac{F}{P}\right)^{1/T} - 1 \qquad (2.6)$$

which must hold because of the no-arbitrage assumption.

This interest rate is known as the *implied repo rate*, because it is similar to a repurchase agreement carried out with the futures market. Generally, a relatively high implied repo rate is indicative of high futures prices, and the same for low implied repo rates. The rates can be used to compare contracts with each other, when these have different terms to maturity and even underlying assets. The implied repo rate for the contract is more stable than the basis; as maturity approaches, the level of the rate becomes very sensitive to changes in the futures price, spot price and (by definition) time to maturity.

2.3 THE BOND BASIS: BASIC CONCEPTS

2.3.1 Introduction

The previous section introduced the no-arbitrage forward pricing principle and the concept of the basis. We will look at this again later. So, we know that the price of an asset, including a bond, that is agreed today for immediate delivery is known as its *spot* price.[9] In essence, the forward price of an asset, agreed today for delivery at some specified future date, is based on the spot price and the cost or income of foregoing delivery until the future date. If an asset carries an income stream, withholding delivery until, say, 3 months in the future, it would present an opportunity cost to an investor in the asset, so the prospective investor would require a discount on the spot price as the price of dealing in a forward. However, if an asset comes with a holding cost – for example, storage costs – then an investor might expect to pay a premium on the spot price, as he would not be incurring the holding costs that are otherwise associated with the asset.

---

[9] We use the term 'immediate' delivery, although for operational, administrative and settlement reasons, actual delivery may be a short period in the future: say, anything up to several days or even longer.

Commodities such as wheat or petroleum are good examples of assets whose forward delivery is associated with a holding cost. For a commodity whose price is agreed today but for which delivery is taken at a forward date, economic logic dictates that the futures price must exceed the spot price. That is, a commodity basis is usually negative. Financial assets such as bonds have zero storage costs, as they are held in electronic form in a clearing system such as CREST, the settlement system for UK gilts;[10] moreover, they provide an income stream that would offset the cost of financing a bond-holding until a future date. Under most circumstances when the yield curve is positively sloping, the holding of a bond position until delivery at a future date will generate a net income to the holder. For these and other reasons it is common for the bond basis to be positive, as the futures price is usually below the spot price.

As we have noted, bond futures contracts do not specify a particular bond, rather a generic or *notional* bond. The actual bond that is delivered against an expired futures contract is the one that makes the cost of delivering it as low as possible. The bond that is selected is known as the cheapest-to-deliver. Considerable research has been undertaken into the concept of the *cheapest-to-deliver* (*CTD*) bond. In fact, certain commodity contracts also trade with an underlying CTD. Burghardt *et al.* (1994) point out that wheat is not an homogenous product, as

---

[10] CREST itself was formed by a merger of the equity settlement system of the same name and the Bank of England's gilt settlement system known as the Central Gilts Office (*CGO*). CREST merged with Euroclear, the international settlement system owned by a consortium of banks, in 2002.

wheat from one part of the country exhibits different characteristics from wheat from another part of the country, and may have to be transported a longer distance (hence at greater cost) to delivery. Therefore, a wheat contract is also priced based on the designated cheapest-to-deliver. There is no physical location factor with government bonds, but futures contracts specify that any bond may be delivered that falls into the required maturity period.

In this section we look at the basic concepts necessary for an understanding of the bond basis, and introduce all the key topics. Basis trading itself is the simultaneous trading of the cash bond and the bond futures contract, an arbitrage trade that seeks to exploit any mis-pricing of the future against the cash or *vice versa*.[11] In liquid and transparent markets such mis-pricing is rare, of small magnitude and very short-lived. The arbitrageur will therefore also try to make a gain from the difference between the costs of holding (or shorting) a bond against that of delivering (or taking delivery of) it at the futures expiry date: essentially, then, the difference between the bond's running yield and its repo financing cost. We'll save the trading principles for Chapter 3. First, let us introduce some basic terminology.

2.3.2   Futures contract specifications

When speaking of bond futures contracts people generally think of the US Treasury bond contract, the Bund

---

[11] Another term for basis trading is *cash-and-carry* trading. The terms are used interchangeably.

contract or the long gilt contract, but then it does depend in which market one is working in or researching. The contract specifications for two of these contracts were given in the last chapter; Table 2.2 reprises them as traded on CBOT and the two European contracts as traded on LIFFE.

Remember that a futures contract is a standardised forward contract, traded on an organised exchange. So the bond futures contracts described in Table 2.2 represent a forward trade in the underlying cash bond. Only a small minority of the futures contracts traded are actually held through to delivery (unlike the case for say, agricultural commodity contracts), but if one does hold a long position at any time in the delivery month, there is a possibility that one will be delivered into.

The notional coupon in the contract specification has relevance in that it is the basis of the calculation of each bond's *price factor* or *conversion factor*; otherwise, it has no bearing on understanding the price behaviour of the futures contract. Remember the contract is based on a *notional* bond, as there will be more than one bond that is eligible for delivery into the contract. The set of deliverable bonds is known as the *delivery basket*. Therefore, the futures price is not based on one particular bond, but acts rather like a hybrid of all the bonds in the basket (see Burghardt *et al.*, 1994, p. 4). What can we say about Table 2.2? For instance, exchanges specify minimum price movements, which is 0.01 for European contracts and 1/32nd for the US contracts.

Table 2.2 Selected futures contract specifications.

Term	Treasury Bond (CBOT)	5-Year Note (CBOT)	Long Gilt (LIFFE)	Bund (LIFFE)
Unit of trading	$100,000 nominal value	$100,000 nominal value	£100,000 nominal value	€100,000 nominal value
Underlying bond	US Treasury bond with a minimum of 15 years remaining to maturity	Original issue US Treasury note with an original maturity of not more than 5.25 years and not less than 4.25 years	UK Gilt with notional 6% coupon and term to maturity of 8.75–13 years	German government bond with 6% coupon and remaining term to maturity of 8.5–10.5 years
Delivery months	March, June, September, December	March, June, September, December	March, June, September, December	March, June, September, December
First notice day			Two business days prior to first day of delivery month	
Last notice day			First business day after last trading day	
Delivery day	Any business day during delivery month		Any business day in delivery month (at seller's choice)	Tenth calendar day of delivery month. If not a business day in Frankfurt, the following Frankfurt business day

Last trading day	12:00 noon on the 8th to the last business day of the delivery month	12:00 noon on the 8th to the last business day of the delivery month	11:00 two business days prior to the last business day in the delivery month	12:30 two Frankfurt business days prior to the delivery day
Last delivery day	Last business day of the delivery month	Last business day of the delivery month		
Price quotation	Points and 32nds of a point per $100 nominal	Points and 32nds of a point per $100 nominal	Per £100 nominal	Per €100 nominal
Tick size and value	1/32nd of a point ($31.25)	1.2 of 1/32nd of a point ($15.625)	0.01 (£10)	0.01 (€10)
Daily price limit	3 points	3 points		
Trading hours	7:20 a.m.–2:00 p.m. (Pit) 5:20 p.m.–8:05 p.m. (CST) 10:30 p.m.–6:00 a.m. (Globex)	7:20 a.m.–2:00 p.m. (Pit) 5:20 p.m.–8:05 p.m. (CST) 6:20 p.m.–9:05 p.m. (CDST)	08:00–18:00 LIFFE CONNECT	07:00–18:00 LIFFE CONNECT

Notes: All times are local. The notional coupon of the Treasury bond, while deprecated as a concept by some writers, is 6%. It was changed from 8% from the March 2000 contract onwards.

Every bond in the delivery basket will have its own conversion factor, which is intended to compensate for the coupon and timing differences of deliverable bonds. The exchange publishes tables of conversion factors in advance of a contract starting to trade, and these remain fixed for the life of the contract. These numbers will be smaller than 1.0 for bonds having coupons less than the notional coupon for the bond in the contract, and greater than 1.0 otherwise.

The definition of the gilt contract detailed in Table 2.2 calls for the delivery of a UK gilt with an effective maturity of between $8\frac{3}{4}$ to 13 years and a 6% notional coupon. We emphasise that the notional coupon should not be an object of a trader's or investor's focus. It exists simply because there would be problems if the definition of deliverable gilts were restricted solely to those with a coupon of exactly 6%. At times, there may be no bonds having this precise coupon. Where there was one or more such bonds, the size of the futures market in relation to the size of the bond issue would expose the market to price manipulation. To avoid this, futures exchanges design contracts in such a way as to prevent anyone dominating the market. In the case of the long gilt and most similar contracts, this is achieved by allowing the delivery of *any* bond with a sufficient maturity, as we have noted. The holder of a long position in futures would prefer to receive a high-coupon bond with significant accrued interest, while those short of the future would favour delivering a cheaper low-coupon bond shortly after the coupon date. This conflict of interest is resolved by adjusting the *invoice amount*, the amount paid in exchange for the bond, to account for coupon rate and timing of the bond actually delivered.

Equation (2.7) gives this invoice amount:

$$Inv_{amt} = (P_{fut} \times CF) + AI \qquad (2.7)$$

where Inv_{amt} = Invoice amount;
$\quad\quad P_{fut}$ = Futures price;
$\quad\quad CF$ = Conversion factor;
$\quad\quad AI$ = Accrued interest.

We will consider invoice and settlement amounts again later.

2.3.3   The conversion factor

So, we know that a bond futures contract represents any bond whose maturity date falls in the period described in the contract specifications. During the delivery month, and up to the expiry date, the party that is short the future has the option on which bond to deliver and on what day in the month to deliver it. Let us consider the long gilt contract on LIFFE. If we assume the person that is short the future delivers on the expiry date, for each contract they must deliver to the exchange's clearing house £100,000 nominal of a notional 6% gilt of between $8\frac{3}{4}$ and 13 years' maturity.[12] Of course, no such specific bond exists, so the seller delivers a bond from

---

[12] In our example, to the London Clearing House. The *LCH* then on-delivers to the party that is long the contract. The long pays the settlement invoice price.

within the delivery basket. However, if the seller delivers a bond of, say, 5% coupon and 9 years' maturity, intuitively we see that the value of this bond is lower than a 6% bond of 13 years' maturity. While the short future may well think, 'fine by me', the long future will most certainly think not. There would be the same aggrieved feelings, just reversed, if the seller was required to deliver a bond of 7% coupon. To equalise all bonds, irrespective of which actual bond is delivered, the futures exchange assigns a *conversion factor* to each bond in the delivery basket. This serves to make the delivery acceptable to both parties. Conversion factors are used in the invoice process to calculate the value of the delivered bond that is equal to that specified by the contract. In some texts the conversion factor is known as the *price factor*. The concept of the conversion factor was developed by CBOT in the 1970s.

Table 2.3 shows the conversion factors for all gilts that were eligible for delivery for the December 2000 to March 2002 contracts. Notice how the conversion factors exhibit the 'pull to par', decreasing towards 1.00 for those with a coupon above the notional 7% and increasing towards 1.00 for bonds with a coupon below 7%. The passage of time also shows bonds falling out of the delivery basket, and the introduction of a new issue into the basket, the 5% gilt maturing 7 March 2012.

The yield obtainable on bonds that have different coupons but identical maturities can be equalised by adjusting the price for each bond. This principle is used to calculate the conversion factors for different

Table 2.3 Conversion factors for deliverable gilts, Dec00 to Mar02 long gilt contracts.

| | **Futures contract** | | | | | |
Gilt	Dec00	Mar01	Jun01	Sep01	Dec01	Mar02
5.75% Treasury 2009	0.917 472 8	0.918 980 2				
6.25% Treasury 2010	0.946 747 8	0.947 561 1	0.948 641 5	0.949 495 6	0.950 587 4	
9% Conversion 2011	1.147 928 1	1.145 557 8	1.143 102 6	1.140 593 6	1.138 124 0	1.135 585 9
5% Treasury 2012				0.852 879 1	0.855 172 7	0.857 727 0
9% Treasury 2012	1.157 636 8	1.155 551 2	1.153 162 6			
8% Treasury 2013	1.083 567 6	1.082 620 6	1.081 499 0	1.080 511 4	1.079 356 0	1.078 336 3

Source: LIFFE.

bonds. The conversion factor for a bond is the price per £1 (or per $1, €1 and so on) at which the bond would give a yield equal to the yield of the notional coupon specified in the futures contract. This is 7% in the case of the long gilt contract, 6% for the Treasury long bond and so on. In other words, the conversion factor for each bond is the price such that every bond would provide an investor with the same yield if purchased; or, the price at which a deliverable bond would trade if its gross redemption yield was 7% (or 6% and so on). The yield calculation is rounded to whole quarters, given the delivery month cycle of futures. Futures exchanges calculate conversion factors effective either on the exact delivery date, where a single date is defined, or (as at LIFFE) on the 1st day of the delivery month if delivery can take place at any time during the delivery month.

The conversion factor is assigned by the exchange to each bond in the delivery basket at the start of trading of each contract. It remains constant throughout the life of the contract. A particular bond that remains in the delivery basket over a length of time will have different conversion factors for successive contracts. For example, the 9% UK Treasury maturing on 13 October 2008 had conversion factors of 1.145 431 7, 1.142 995 5 and 1.140 715 5 for the LIFFE long gilt contracts that matured in June, September and December 1998, respectively.

Other things being equal, bonds with a higher coupon will have larger conversion factors than those with lower coupons. For bonds with the same coupon, maturity has an influence, though this is slightly less obvious.

For bonds with coupons below the notional rate defined in the contract description, the conversion factor is smaller for bonds with a longer maturity. The opposite is true for bonds carrying coupons in excess of the notional coupon rate, for which the conversion factor will be larger the longer the maturity. This effect arises from the mathematics of fixed-interest securities. Bonds with coupon below current market yields will trade at a discount. This discount is larger the longer the maturity, because it is a disadvantage to hold a bond paying a coupon lower than current market rates, and this disadvantage is greater the longer the period to the bond maturing. Conversely, bonds with coupons above current market yields trade at a premium which will be greater the longer the maturity.

To help calculate the *invoice price* of a bond on delivery, we multiply the price of the final settlement price of the futures contract with its conversion factor. This gives us the *converted price*. The price payable by the long future on delivery of the bond is the invoice price, and this is the futures settlement price plus accrued interest. This was shown in simple fashion as (2.1). The actual invoice price, calculated once the actual bond being delivered is known, is given by:

$$P_{inv} = (M_{fut} \times P_{futsett} \times CF) + AI \qquad (2.8)$$

where P_{inv} = Invoice price;
              M_{fut} = Nominal value of the delivered bonds
                    as specified in the contract;
        $P_{futsett}$ = Futures settlement price.

Invoice amount

When the bond is delivered, the long pays the short an invoice amount:

$$Invoiced = \left(\frac{EDSP}{100 \times CF \times Nominal}\right) + AI \quad (2.9)$$

The settlement price (or *exchange delivery settlement price, EDSP*) is the trading price per £100 nominal for the futures contract on the last day of trading, and is confirmed by the exchange. The invoice amount includes accrued interest because the futures contract is traded at a *clean* price and does not include accrued interest.

Box 2.1   Calculating the invoice price.

A futures contract settles at 102.50. The contract specifies £100,000 nominal of the underlying bond. The delivered bond has a conversion factor of 1.14579 and accrued interest of 0.73973. The settlement price is equal to 1.025% of the nominal value (par value). The invoice price is calculated as:

$$P_{inv} = (100,000 \times 1.025 \times 1.145\,79) + 0.739\,73$$

$$= £117,443 + 0.739\,73$$

For the Treasury long bond the conversion factor is calculated using (2.10):

$$CF = \frac{1}{1.03^{t/6}} \left[\frac{C}{2} + \frac{C}{0.06} \left(1 - \frac{1}{1.03^{2N}}\right) + \frac{1}{1.03^{2N}} \right] \quad (2.10)$$

where N = Complete years to maturity as at the delivery month;

$t =$ Number of months in excess of the whole N (rounded *down* to whole quarters).

The LIFFE conversion factor for the long gilt was given in Appendix 1.A. The formula is actually the same, beginners are invited to explain that this is indeed so. To illustrate (2.10), if a deliverable Treasury bond has a maturity of 19 years and 5 months, t is 3 because the 5 months is rounded down to one quarter or 3 months. Hence, if the maturity is 19 years and 9 months, t is 6.

It is worth summarising what we know so far about conversion factors:

- conversion factors remain constant for a bond from the moment they are assigned to the expiry of the contract;
- conversion factors are different for each bond and for each contract;[13] from Table 2.3, which relates to the long gilt contract and its then notional coupon of 7%, we see that conversion factors for bonds with coupons higher than 7% diminish in value for each successive contract month, while those for bonds with coupons lower than 7% rise in value for successive contract months.[14] This reflects the 'pull to par' effect which for bonds with the higher coupon is falling from a premium and for bonds with the lower coupon is rising from a discount;

---

[13] If two bonds had identical coupons and maturity dates, then they would have the same conversion factor for a specific contract. However, under these terms the two bonds would be identical as well ...

[14] The notional coupon for the long gilt was changed from 7% to 6% in March 2004.

- the conversion factor is used to calculate the invoice price of a bond that is delivered into a futures contract;
- bonds with coupons greater than the notional coupon of the futures contract have a conversion factor higher than 1, while bonds with coupons lower than the notional coupon have a conversion factor lower than 1.

The conversion factor is not a hedge ratio, as has been strongly emphasised by both Burghardt and Kolb,[15] and should not be used as such. Certain textbooks and market practitioners have suggested that using the ratio of two bonds' conversion factors can be an effective hedge ratio for hedging a bond position, rather than the traditional approach of using the ratio of basis point values. This is fallacious and will lead to serious errors. The conversion factor of a bond is influenced primarily by its coupon, whereas the modified duration of a bond – from which is derived the Basis Point Value (BPV) – is a function mainly of its term to maturity. Hence, it is not correct to substitute them. If an investor was hedging a position in a long-dated bond of low coupon, and the current CTD bond was a short-dated bond of high coupon, the volatility ratio calculated using the respective conversion factors would be lower than unity. However, using respective BPVs would result in a volatility ratio higher than 1. This example illustrates how using a ratio of conversion factors can result in serious hedging errors, and this approach must not be adopted.

Using conversion factors provides an effective system

[15] Burghardt *et al.* (1994, p. 9 and ch. 5); Kolb (2000, p. 217).

for making all deliverable bonds perfect substitutes for one another. The system is not perfect, of course. Conversion factors are calculated to equalise returns at a single uniform yield, the notional coupon rate specified in the contract specification. In practice though, bonds trade at different yields, resulting in the yield curve. Hence, despite the use of conversion factors, bonds will not be precisely 'equal' at the time of delivery. Some bonds will be relatively more expensive, some cheaper; one particular bond will be the CTD bond. The CTD bond is an important concept in the pricing of bond futures contracts.

2.3.4 The bond basis

Basis trading arises from the difference between the current clean price of a bond and the (implied) forward clean price at which the bond is bought through the purchase of a futures contract. The difference between these two prices is known as the *gross basis*. This is the bond basis to which the market refers, the difference between the bond's spot cash price and the price implied by the current price of the futures contract. The latter is given by multiplying the futures price by the relevant bond's conversion factor.

The formula for calculating the gross basis is therefore:

$$Basis = P_{bond} - (P_{fut} \times CF) \qquad (2.11)$$

From (2.11) we might think that if we sell a futures contract short, in effect this guarantees an ability to deliver the bond at the futures delivery date and receive a known price for the bond. However, the price payable for the bond at delivery is based on the future's final settlement price, and not the trading price of the future at any time beforehand, and so this thinking is erroneous.

In the Treasury market both cash and futures prices are quoted as points and ticks (32nds) per $100 nominal value, and if necessary as half-ticks or 64ths. A 64th price is indicated by a +.

The gross basis can be explained essentially as the difference between the running yield on the bond and the current repo (money market) rate. However, a residual factor exists due to the delivery option implicit in the design of the futures contract and to the daily marking-to-market of the contract, both of which are more difficult to quantify. This residual amount is known as the *net basis*. Net basis is the gross basis adjusted for net carry. Net carry is the actual coupon income and re-investment less borrowing expense, which is at the security's actual repo or money market financing rate.

Figure 2.6 is the Bloomberg page DLV of the deliverable bonds for the June 2000 long gilt contract, and shows the conversion factors and gross basis value for each bond in the basket.

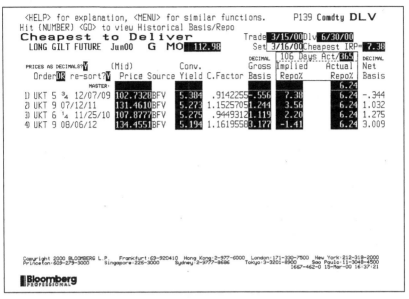

Figure 2.6 Delivery basket for Jun00 long gilt, Bloomberg page DLV, 15 March 2000.

© Bloomberg L.P. Used with permission. Visit *www.bloomberg.com*

Box 2.2   The gross basis

Consider the following market details, all relating to one instantaneous point in time:

Settlement date	16 March 2000
Futures delivery date	30 June 2000
Days to delivery	106
Bond price (UKT 9% 2011)	131.4610
Accrued interest	1.578 082 2
Accrued to delivery	4.191 780 8
Futures price (M0 LIFFE long gilt)	112.98
Conversion factor	1.152 570 5
Cash market repo rate	6.24%

We can calculate the gross basis that would apply in a hypothetical cash-and-carry trade, where there is a simultaneous purchase of the bond and sale of the futures contract as shown below.

Bond purchase – outflow of funds:

$$131.461 + 1.578\,1 = 133.039\,082\,2$$

Futures sale – inflow of funds:

$$(112.98 \times 1.152\,570\,5) + 4.192 = 134.409\,19\,6$$

The gross basis is:

$$131.461\,0 - (112.98 \times 1.152\,570\,5)$$

or $1.243\,584\,91$.

2.3.5 The net basis

We've seen from the previous section that gross basis measures the carry on a bond that applies during the life of the futures contract. Because of other factors associated with the delivery into a futures contract, principally that delivery is at the option of the short future, the gross basis is not the actual carry that would be incurred if a trader put on a cash versus futures trade. This is measured by the *net basis*. The net basis causes much confusion amongst market participants, but it is a straightforward concept. Burghardt *et al.* (1994) state that the net basis is the difference between a bond's basis and its total carry to delivery.[16] Plona describes net basis as the difference between the *implied repo rate* (*IRR*) and the general collateral repo rate. We consider the IRR in Section 2.3.6.[17]

Both descriptions are good ways in which to consider net basis. Essentially, the net basis is the gross basis adjusted for net carry. Net carry is the actual coupon income (and

---

[16] Burghardt *et al.* (1994, p. 33). It is also known as the *basis net of carry*.
[17] Plona (1997, p. 32).

any re-investment income) minus borrowing expense, which is at the security's actual repo (money market) rate. The net basis is therefore the true 'economic basis' and measures the net gain from a simultaneous position in the cash bond and the futures contract. A positive value represents a *loss* or net cost to the long cash/short futures position, and the net basis is the expected *profit* for the short cash/long futures position (where the actual repo rate used is the reverse repo rate). The opposite is true for negative net basis values.

The net basis is calculated on the assumption that a basis trade is conducted by the arbitrageur borrowing funds to purchase the CTD bond, financing it in the repo market, and shorting the futures contract. It measures the maximum *loss* that would be suffered by holding this position until the contract expiry date. The net basis should be negative as a loss measure; a positive net basis indicates the potential profit from such a trade.[18] On the other hand, a negative net basis theoretically indicates the potential profit from a short bond/long futures position.

To calculate the net basis, we need to make an assumption about the financing rates that would apply to a basis trade.[19] This centres on the repo rate that is applicable to

---

[18] Note that in some cases and vendor systems the net basis appears to be positive because the negative sign is left off, under the assumption that users are aware that the net basis represents the loss from a long cash/short futures trade.

[19] As we shall see in Section 2.3.6, no assumptions need to be made when determining the IRR, which is calculated from actual market-observed prices.

the cash bond element of the trade. Analysts use one of two methods:

- the specific repo rate for the cash bond, fixed to the maturity date. This is a logical approach, as it provides an accurate measure of the financing cost associated with running a long position in the bond, and then delivering it into the futures exchange. Calculating net basis under this method provides a measure of the value of the delivery option;
- the overnight *general collateral* (*GC*) repo rate, assuming therefore that the bond position is financed on a daily basis. Assuming that the overnight rate will be maintained more or less over the term of the trade is risky.

Box 2.3 illustrates the calculation of the net basis.

Box 2.3   The net basis.

Consider this calculation for the June 1998 long gilt future contract. At this time the 'special ex' rule applies to delivery of bonds into the contract, something that no longer applied with the removal of special ex-trading in August 1998.

Trade date	24 April 1998
Settlement date	25 April 1998
M8 long gilt future price	109.656 25
CTD bond ($8\frac{1}{2}$% Treasury 2007)	106.343 75
Accrued interest	2.305 48
Accrued to delivery	3.423 288 2
Dirty price	108.649 32
Conversion factor ($8\frac{1}{2}$% 2007)	0.967 406 4
Repo rate	6.36%

The converted price of the bond (that is, through the futures contract) is:

$$109.656\,25 \times 0.967\,406\,4 = 106.082\,16$$

The market clean price is 106.343 75, therefore the gross basis is:

$$106.343\,75 - 106.082\,16 = 0.261\,59$$

Due to the special-ex rule in this case, the last day for delivery of $8\frac{1}{2}\%$ Treasury 2007 into the futures contract is 12 June. This makes the term 48 days. The total price paid including accrued interest will be 108.649 23. To finance that using repo for 48 days until 12 June will cost £0.908 724 3. The holder of the gilt will however earn 48 days' accrued interest of £1.117 808 2. Therefore, buying the bond direct gives the owner an income advantage of £0.209 083 9.

The difference between the gross basis and this income advantage is £0.216 159 – £0.209 083 9, that is £0.0525. It therefore represents the gain by buying the gilt using the futures contract rather than buying directly in the market.

Of course, the long gilt contract gives the futures seller the right to deliver any of the gilts in the delivery basket and on any day of the delivery month. If the CTD is bought through a futures contract the buyer may find that, because of market movements, a different gilt is delivered. The short future in effect holds an option which decreases the value of the futures contract to the long.

For this reason the *net* basis is usually positive. The futures contract is also marked-to-market which means that the gain or loss on the contract is spread over the life of the contract, in contrast to a forward contract. This effect is small but will again lead to the net basis differing from 0.

The net basis is given by:

$$Net\ Basis = \left(108.649\,23 \times \left(1 + 6.36 \times \frac{48}{36\,500} \right) \right)$$

$$- \left((109.656\,25 \times 0.967\,406\,4) + 3.423\,882 \right)$$

$$= 109.557\,954\,3 - 109.505\,446\,25$$

$$= 0.052\,508\,05$$

2.3.6   The implied repo rate

In a basis trade the rate implied by the strategy is known as a repo rate because it is equivalent to a *repurchase agreement* with the futures market. In effect, the short future lends money to the futures market: the short future agrees to buy a bond with a simultaneous provision to sell it back to the market at a predetermined price and to receive a rate of interest on his money, the repo rate. It is the *implied repo rate* because it is an expected repo rate gain if the trade was carried out. In some literature it is suggested as a complex and obscure calculation; in fact, the Implied Repo Rate (IRR) is very straightforward to calculate. It is the theoretical return from a basis trade of long cash bond against short future, with the bond delivered into the future on expiry.

The IRR is a measure of return from a basis trade. Consider the cash flows involved when one is long bond/ short future. We have:

- a cash outflow from purchasing the bond;
- a cash inflow on delivery into the future, including the accrued interest to the delivery date;
- the cash borrowed to finance the trade.

We simply therefore wish to have the percentage return of the investment over the borrowing cost. That is:

$$IRR = \frac{((P_{futs} \times CF) + AI_{del}) - (P_{bond} + AI)}{P_{bond} + AI} \times \frac{M}{Days} \quad (2.12)$$

where $M =$ Day-base, either 360 or 365;
         $Days =$ Term of the trade.

There is no need to remember this version though, Burghardt *et al.* (1994, p. 14) simplify it to:

$$IRR = \left[\frac{P_{invoice} - P_{bond}}{P_{bond}}\right] \times \left(\frac{360}{n}\right) \qquad (2.13)$$

which is identical to (2.12), with n for the number of days to delivery, and all prices still include accrued interest, at the time of the trade (bond) or to delivery (future). The formula written as (2.13) is easy to explain. The invoice price is the futures invoice price, the amount from the delivery on expiry. Of course, the actual invoice price is a function of the final futures settlement price, but we adjust the current futures price with the conversion factor to allow for this.

Note that Bloomberg quotes the formula in still more simplified fashion, as:

$$IRR = \left[\frac{P_{FutsInvoice}}{P_{bond}} - 1\right] \times \left(\frac{360}{n}\right) \qquad (2.14)$$

with the 360-day base associated with the US Treasury market.

Both (2.12) and (2.13) assume that no coupon is paid during the trade. If a coupon is paid during the trade, it is considered as being reinvested, and the cash flow total must therefore include both the coupon and the reinvestment income generated. The re-investment rate used in the market is one of the following:

- the implied repo rate;
- the bond's yield-to-maturity. This is described as being consistent with the bond yield calculation itself, which assumes reinvestment of coupon at the bond yield;
- the overnight repo rate, and rolled over. This is justified on the basis that traders in fact do not reinvest the coupon but use the cash to reduce funding costs.

The first two are assumed to apply to maturity, while the second must be calculated at the prevailing rate each day. If the reinvestment rate is assumed to be the IRR, it is the rate that results in:

$$P_{bond} \times \left(1 + IRR\left(\frac{n}{M}\right)\right) = P_{invoice} + \left(\frac{C}{2}\right) \times \left[1 + IRR\left(\frac{n_2}{M}\right)\right]$$

(2.15)

where n_2 is the number of days between the coupon payment and the futures expiry (delivery) date. Expression (2.15) is then rearranged for the IRR, to give us:

$$IRR = \frac{\left(P_{invoice} + \dfrac{C}{2} - P_{bond}\right) \times M}{(P_{bond} \times n) - \left(\dfrac{C}{2} \times n_2\right)}$$

(2.16)

The deliverable bond that has the highest IRR is the *cheapest-to-deliver* bond or *CTD*. We see from (2.16) that the IRR is a function of the bond price, the value of which is compared to the forward price for the bond implied by futures price. As such the status of the CTD bond reflects the bond's price (in other words, its yield).

If the yield of a bond within the delivery basket moves sufficiently *vis-à-vis* the other deliverable bonds, it may become the CTD bond. A change in the cheapest bond is an important development and any such change should be anticipated in advance by good traders.

The bond with the highest IRR will, almost invariably, have the lowest net basis. On rare occasions this will not be observed. When two bonds each have IRRs that are very similar, it is sometimes the case that the bond with the (slightly) lower IRR has a (slightly) lower net basis.

The CTD bond is just that: it is the cheapest bond to deliver into the futures contract in terms of running costs. The short future has the delivery option, and will elect to deliver the CTD bond unless there is a reason it cannot, in which case it will deliver the next cheapest at greater cost to itself. Assuming that a basis trade is put on with the CTD bond against the future, if the CTD changes then the position becomes useless and will be unwound at great loss. The CTD bond is what the market will treat as the actual underlying bond of the futures contract, and it is closely observed. Pricing theory informs us that the futures price will track the CTD bond price; in fact, it is the other way around, with the liquidity and transparency of the futures contract and its price meaning that the CTD bond price tracks that of the future. Under the terms of the long gilt contract, the CTD gilt can be delivered on any business day of the delivery month, but in practice only one of two days are ever used to make delivery: the first (business) day of the delivery month or the last (delivery) day of the month. If the current yield on the CTD gilt exceeds the money market repo rate, the bond will be delivered on the last business day of the month, because the short future earns more by holding on to the bond than by delivering it and investing the proceeds in the money market; otherwise, the bond will be delivered on the first business day of the delivery month. Until very recently a gilt that was eligible for trading *special ex-dividend* on any day of the delivery month was not eligible for delivery into that gilt contract. However, from August 1998 the provision for special ex-dividend trading was removed from gilts, so this consideration no longer applies. Other gilts that are not eligible for delivery are index-linked, partly paid or convertible gilts.[20] For gilts the IRR for all deliverable bonds can be calculated using (2.12) in the normal way. However, if a bond goes ex-dividend between trade date and delivery date, a modification is required in which the interest accrued is negative during the ex-dividend period.

---

[20] Gilts go ex-dividend 7 business days before the coupon date, this being the record date to determine the investors that will receive the coupon. Prior to its withdrawal, counterparties could agree between themselves to trade ex-dividend up to 2 weeks before the ex-dividend date, this being known as *special ex-dividend*. During trading for the September 1997 long gilt contract, some market participants forgot (or were unaware) that gilts that were special ex-dividend at any time during the delivery month became ineligible for delivery, and had traded in the current CTD bond – the 9% 2008 – under the assumption that they could deliver, or would be delivered into, this bond. When the CTD bond changed it resulted in losses for parties that had not been aware of this. This despite the fact that LIFFE sent out a notice informing the market that the CTD for September 1997 would not be the 9% 2008 for this reason ...

Box 2.4   The implied repo rate.

Another way of looking at the concept of the CTD bond is in terms of the IRR. The CTD bond is the bond that gives the highest IRR to the short from a cash-and-carry trade; that is, a strategy of buying the bond (with borrowed funds) in the cash market and selling it forward into the futures market. The bond is funded in the repo market, and by selling it forward the trade is in effect a repo with the futures market, hence *implied* repo rate.

To illustrate we calculate the IRR for the 9% Treasury 2008, a UK gilt, at the time that the 'front month' contract was the December 1998 contract. The price of the gilt is 129.083 4. The December 1998 long gilt futures contract is trading at 114.50. The date is 1 October. The money market rate on this date is 7.25%. As the current (or *running*) yield on the 9% 2008, at 6.972%, is lower than the money market rate, it will be delivered at the beginning of December (that is, in 61 days from now). To identify the CTD bond we would need to calculate the IRR for all eligible bonds. We use the conversion factor for the bond which is 1.140 715, calculated and given out by LIFFE before the futures contract began trading.

The cash outflow in a cash-and-carry trade is:

Bond dirty price	129.083 4
Interest cost (1 October–	
1 December)	$129.083\,4 \times (0.072\,5 \times (61/365))$
Total outflow	130.647 4

The bond (whose price includes 171 days' accrued interest on 1 October) has to be financed at the money market rate of 7.25% for the 61 days between 1 October and 1 December, when the bond (if it is still the CTD) is delivered into the futures market.

The cash inflow per £100 nominal as a result of this trade is:

Implied clean price of bond on	
1 December (futures price on	
1 October multiplied by	
conversion factor)	$114.50 \times 1.140\,715\,5$

Accrued interest
  (1 October–1 December)   £9 × (61/365)
  Total inflow   132.11603

The implied price of the bond on 1 December equals the futures price on 1 October multiplied by the conversion factor for the bond. Because the futures price is quoted clean, accrued interest has to be added to obtain the implied dirty price on 1 December.

This cash-and-carry trade which operates for 61 days from 1 October to 1 December generates a rate of return or IRR of:

$$IRR = \left(\frac{132.116\,03 - 130.647\,4}{130.647\,4}\right) \times \frac{365}{61} \times 100$$

$$= 6.726\%$$

Box 2.5 Calculating gross basis, net basis and implied repo rate.

The gross basis is the difference between the actual price of the bond and the forward price of the bond as implied by the price of the futures contract, and represents the carrying cost of the bond. This is the actual difference between the coupon gain and re-investment minus the carry costs (which is at the actual money market repo rate). A positive net basis represents the loss that would result from a long cash/short futures position, and therefore the theoretical gain from a short cash/long futures trade, where the actual repo rate is the reverse repo rate transacted when covering the short cash position. The IRR is the theoretical return from a long cash/short futures trade, assuming that the trader is short the number of futures equal to the bond's conversion factor for each £100,000 nominal of bonds held. Any coupon payments are assumed to be reinvested at the IRR.

Earlier in this book we presented the formulae for gross basis and IRR. The net basis is given by:

$$\text{Net basis} = \left(P_{bond} \times \left(1 + r \times \frac{Del}{36\,500}\right)\right) - ((P_{fut} \times CF) + AI_{del})$$

where P_{bond} = Bond dirty price;
          r = Actual repo rate (expressed as per cent × 100);

Del = Days to delivery;
P_{fut} = Futures price;
CF = Bond's conversion factor;
AI_{del} = Bond's accrued interest to delivery.

For net basis calculations in Treasury or euro markets the appropriate 360-day basis is used.

The calculations are for the CTD bond for the long gilt contract, which was the $6\frac{1}{4}\%$ 2010 gilt. We use mid prices for the bond. The trade is buying the cash and simultaneously selling the future. Note that gilts accrue on actual/actual basis and there were 184 days in the interest period 25 May–25 November 2001. The accrued interest calculation is therefore $(80/184 \times (6.25 \times 0.5))$ for the first date and $(126/184 \times (6.25 \times 0.5))$ for the delivery date.

Settlement date	13 August 2001
Futures price	115.94
$6\frac{1}{4}\%$ Treasury 25/11/2010 price	110.20
Conversion factor	0.949 495 6
Repo rate	4.90%

Calculations

Cash out on 13/8/2001:

$$110.20 \text{ plus accrued } (80 \text{ days}) = 111.558\,696$$

Cash in on 28/9/2021:

$$(115.94 \times 0.949\,495\,6) \text{ plus accrued} = 110.084\,52 + 2.139\,946$$

$$(46 \text{ days later})$$

$$= 112.224\,465\,9$$

Gross basis

$$110.20 - 110.084\,519\,9 = \mathbf{0.115\,480\,1}$$

Net basis

$$\left(111.558\,696 \times \left(1 + 4.90 \times \frac{46}{36\,500}\right)\right) - 112.224\,465\,9$$

$$= \mathbf{0.023\,143\,2}$$

Implied repo rate

$$\left(\frac{112.224\,465\,9}{111.558696} - 1 \right) \times \frac{365}{46} \times 100 = \textbf{4.735\,390\%}$$

These calculations are confirmed by looking at the Bloomberg screens YA and DLV for value on 13 August 2001, as shown in Figures 2.7 and 2.8, respectively. Figure 2.7 is selected for the $6\frac{1}{4}\%$ 2010 gilt and Figure 2.8 is selected for the front month contract at the time, the Sep01 gilt future. Figure 2.9 shows the change in CTD bond status between the $6\frac{1}{4}\%$ 2010 gilt and the 9% 2011 gilt, the second cheapest bond at the time of the analysis, with changes in the futures price. The change of CTD status with changes in the IRR is shown in Figure 2.10. Both are Bloomberg page HCG.

Page DLV on Bloomberg lists deliverable bonds for any selected futures contract. Bonds are listed in order of declining *implied repo rate*; the user can select in increasing or decreasing order of implied repo rate, basis, yield, maturity, coupon or duration. The user can also select the price source for the bonds (in our example set at 'Bloomberg Generic' rather than any specific bank or market maker) and the current cash repo rate.

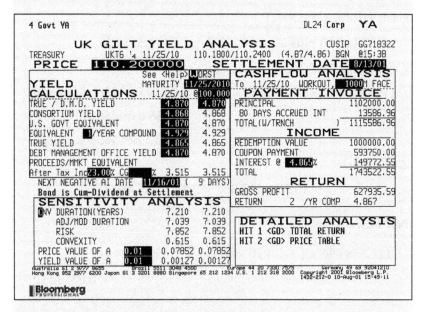

Figure 2.7 Bloomberg YA page for $6\frac{1}{4}\%$ 2010 gilt, showing accrued interest for value 13 August 2001.

© Bloomberg L.P. Used with permission. Visit *www.bloomberg.com*

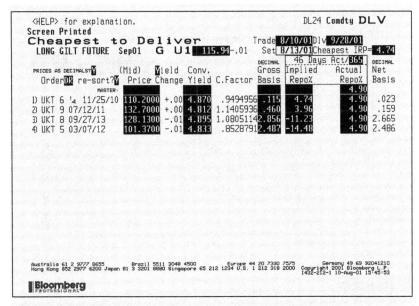

Figure 2.8 Bloomberg DLV page for Sep01 (U1) gilt contract, showing gross basis, net basis and IRR for trade date 12 August 2001.

© Bloomberg L.P. Used with permission. Visit *www.bloomberg.com*

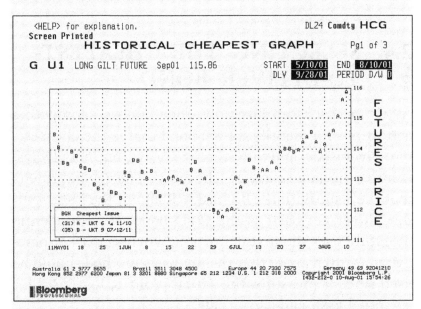

Figure 2.9 Bloomberg HCG page for Sep01 (U1) gilt contract, showing CTD bond history up to 12 August 2001 with changes in futures price.

© Bloomberg L.P. Used with permission. Visit *www.bloomberg.com*

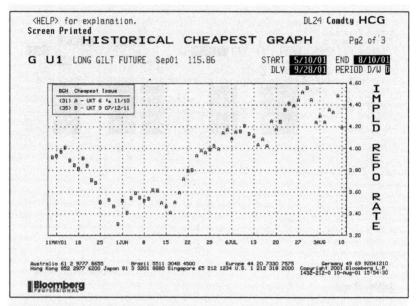

Figure 2.10 Bloomberg HCG page for Sep01 (U1) gilt contract, showing CTD bond history up to 12 August 2001, with changes in IRR.

© Bloomberg L.P. Used with permission. Visit *www.bloomberg.com*

2.4 SELECTING THE CHEAPEST-TO-DELIVER BOND

As we've discussed just now, there are two competing definitions for identifying the bond that is the cheapest-to-deliver issue, and they almost always, but not always, identify the same issue as 'cheapest'. The general rule is that the issue with the highest IRR and/or the issue with the lowest net basis is the CTD bond. Most academic literature uses the first definition, whereas market practitioners often argue that the net basis method should be used since it measures the actual profit & loss (p&l) for an actual cash-and-carry trade.

It is up to the individual trader to decide which method to use as the basis for analysis. For example, Bloomberg terminals use the IRR method. The justification for this is that many market participants accept that the IRR method is appropriate to the cash-and-carry investor seeking maximum return per dollar invested. The main area of disagreement regards those cases where an arbitrageur finances (repos) the cash side of the trade and the net basis measures their resulting profit or loss. In a Bloomberg analysis this net basis is presented as percentage points of par (the same units as price), although some practitioners express it as p&l per million bonds. It is primarily because the net basis is per par amount rather than per pound invested that the two methods occasionally identify different 'cheapest' issues. Note that in practice net basis will always be a loss, otherwise traders would arbitrage an infinite amount of any issue with a profitable net basis. Therefore, the basis method identifies the issue which has the *smallest loss* per million pounds nominal as the cheapest issue.

The only reason a trader is willing to accept this guaranteed loss is that they don't intend to follow through exactly with this trade to maturity. Being long of the basis – that is, short futures – essentially gives the trader numerous delivery and trading options; the cost of these is the net basis that the trader pays. In effect, the trader is buying options for the cost of the net basis. The number of options they buy is indicated by the *conversion factor* since that is the hedge factor for the cheapest issue. Therefore, the cost per option is the net basis divided by the conversion factor. When ranked by net basis per contract – that is, divided by the conversion factor – the cheapest by this method invariably agrees with the IRR method.

2.5 TRADING THE BASIS

2.5.1 The basis position

Basis trading or cash-and-carry trading is an arbitrage-driven activity that involves the simultaneous trading of cash bonds and exchange-traded bond futures contracts. Traders speak of going 'long the basis' or of 'buying the basis' when they buy the bond and sell the future. The equivalent number of futures contracts to trade per 100,000 nominal value of cash bond is given by the conversion factor. The opposite position, buying the future and selling the cash bond, is known as 'selling the basis' or 'going short the basis'. Someone who is long the basis has bought the basis itself (hence the expression!) and will therefore profit if the basis increases – that is, the price of the bond increases relative to the price of the futures contract.[21] A trader who has sold the basis will gain if the basis decreases – that is, the price of the bond falls relative to the futures contract price.

Ideally, each side of the position will be executed simultaneously, and most derivatives exchanges have a basis trading facility that enables a party to undertake this.

---

[21] Remember, when we say the price of the future, we mean the price as adjusted by the relevant conversion factor.

Certain government bond primary dealers will quote a price in the basis as well. If this is not possible, the trade can be put on separately, known as 'legging into the trade' as each leg is carried out at different times. To do this, generally the cash bond position is put on first and then the futures position, as the latter is more liquid and transparent. Whichever way round the trade is effected though, this method carries with it some risk, as the price of the leg yet to be traded can move against you, complicating the completion of the trade.[22] If this happens there is a danger that the second leg is put on one or two ticks offside, and straight away the trade starts off at a loss. This should be avoided if at all possible. There is also a bid–offer spread to take into account, for both cash and future positions.

The arbitrageur hopes to generate profit from a basis trade, and this will be achieved from changes in the basis itself and/or gains from the funding or carry. If the net funding cost is positive, then this will add to any profit or reduce losses arising from changes in the basis. This is where the repo rate comes in. The trader may elect to fund the bond position, whether long or short, in overnight repo but generally the best approach is to fix a term repo, with expiry date matching the date at which the trader hopes to unwind the trade. This may be to the contract expiry date or before. If short the basis, it is vital that the repo desk is aware if there is any

---

[22] From personal experience the author will testify that this is an extremely stressful position to be in! Don't leg into the trade unless there is no alternative.

chance that the bond goes special, as this could prove costly unless the repo is fixed to the trade maturity. There is also a bid–offer spread to consider with the repo rate, and while this is usually quite small for GC repo – say, as little as 3 basis points – it may be wider for specifics, from 10 to 20 basis points.

In Chapter 3 we consider further issues in trading the basis.

Box 2.6   A summary of the basic position.

Cash-and-carry trading

In this trade, we undertake simultaneous transactions in:

- buying the cash bond;
- selling the bond futures contract.

The trader buys the cheapest-to-deliver bond, the financing of which is fixed in the repo market (trader pays the repo rate). The trader believes that the bond is cheaper in the cash market than its forward price implied by the price of the futures contract. On the expiry date of the futures contract, any bond in the deliverable basket is eligible for delivery, but (assuming no change in CTD status) the trader will deliver the bond they are long of. The trader's potential gain arises from the mis-pricing of the bond in the cash market.

Reverse cash-and-carry trading

In this trade we undertake simultaneous transactions by:

- selling the CTD bond in the cash market, and covering the position by entering into reverse repo (the trader receives the repo rate);
- buying the equivalent number of futures contracts.

For the reverse basis trade to generate profit there can be no change in the CTD status of the bond; if another bond becomes the CTD at contract expiry, a loss will result. On futures expiry,

the trader is delivered into the bond in which they have a short position, and this also enables them to close out the repo trade. Theoretical profit is generated because the invoice price paid for the bond is lower than the price received at the start of the trade in the cash market, once funding costs have been taken into account.

2.6 EXERCISES

1 The gilt future is trading at 114.55. Which of the following gilts is the cheapest-to-deliver?

Bond	Price	Conversion factor
9% 2008	130.718 8	1.140 715 5
7% 2007	116.375	1.016 526 6
8% 2009	125.437 5	1.075 010 6
9% 2011	136.153 6	1.165 546 5

2 A bond desk puts on an arbitrage trade consisting of a long cash and short futures position. What risks does this trade expose the desk to?

3 Assume that the cheapest-to-deliver bond for a futures contract has a coupon of 6% and has precisely 9 years to maturity. Its price is 103.5625. If its conversion factor is 0.901 235 64, what is the current price of the futures contract?

4 Assess the following market information and determine if there is an arbitrage opportunity available for undertaking a basis trade:

Bond coupon:	8.875%
Maturity:	December 2003
Price:	102.71
Accrued interest:	3.599
Futures price:	85.31
Conversion factor:	1.203 057 68
Repo rate:	6.803%
Days to delivery:	23
Contract size:	100,000
Accrued interest on delivery:	4.182

5 The terms of the LIFFE long gilt contract state that delivery may take place on any day during the delivery month. On 30 May 1999 the yield on the cheapest-to-deliver gilt is 5.716% while the repo rate is 6.24%. On what day will a short future deliver the bond if (i) he already owns the cash bond, (ii) if he does not yet own the bond? Explain your answer.

6 Will there be any change in the current cheapest-to-deliver bond if there is a parallel shift in the yield curve of 50 basis points?

7 The first day of trading of a new futures contract is about to commence. What is the fair price of the contract?

8 Consider the following market data, with price for UK gilts and the LIFFE long gilt contract. Gilts pay semi-annual coupon on an act/act basis.

		Conversion factor
UKT 5.75% 7 Dec 2009	£102.732 8	0.914 225 5
UKT 6.25% 25 Nov 2010	107.8777	0.944 931 2
UKT 9% 6 Aug 2012	134.455 1	1.161 955 8
Futures price	112.98	
Settlement date	16 March 2000	
Futures expiry	30 June 2000	
Actual repo rate	6.24%	

Using this data, calculate the gross basis, the net basis and the implied repo rate for each bond. Which bond is the cheapest-to-deliver? Relative to the futures contract, what is the difference in price between the cheapest-to-deliver bond and the most expensive-to-deliver bond? What does a negative net basis indicate?

9 We wish to determine by how much the yield of a deliverable bond would have to change in order for it to become the cheapest-to-deliver bond. How could we do this?

10 A junior trader feels that there are some arbitrage opportunities available in the basis, which is net positive for the cheapest-to-deliver bond, if he puts on a strategy of long futures versus short in the cheapest-to-deliver. What factors may contribute to prevent her realising a profit equal to the current value of the net basis?

11 A long bond futures contract matures in 56 days, and its current price is 107.55. The price of the cheapest-to-deliver is 129.875, and it has a coupon of 9% and accrued interest of 79 days (act/act). What is the implied repo rate?

12 Discuss the relative merits of analysing the CTD bond using the net basis method against the IRR method.

13 On 19 January 2006 we observe the following:

Settlement date	20 January 2006
Futures price	115.07
UK gilt 8% 2015 price	132.31
Conversion factor	1.146 092 8
Repo rate	4.58%

With regard to the Mar06 long gilt future, which has a last delivery day of 31 Mar 2006, calculate the net basis for this bond. Its coupon dates are 7 June and 7 December.

If the UKT 8.75% 2017, which has coupon dates of 25 February and 25 August, is trading at a price of 143.43 and has a conversion factor of 1.225 934 0, what is its net basis?

Which bond is the CTD?

14 What is contango and backwardation?

15 Is the basis for physically-delivered commodities usually expected to be negative or positive? Explain your answer. What is the position for financial instruments such as bonds?

SELECTED BIBLIOGRAPHY

Benninga, S. and Z. Weiner (1999) An investigation of cheapest-to-deliver on Treasury bond futures contracts. *Journal of Computational Finance* **2**, 39–56.

Boyle, P. (1989) The quality option and the timing option in futures contracts. *Journal of Finance* **44**, 101–113.

Burghardt, G. *et al.* (1994) *The Treasury Bond Basis* (revised edition). Richard D. Irwin.

Fabozzi, F. (1998) *Treasury Securities and Derivatives*. FJF Associates.

Fabozzi, F. (2001) *Bond Portfolio Management* (2nd edition). FJF Associates, chaps 6, 17.

Jonas, S. (1991) 'The change in the cheapest-to-deliver in bond and note futures'. In: R. Dattatreya (ed.), *Fixed Income Analytics*. McGraw-Hill.

Plona, C. (1997) *The European Bond Basis*. McGraw-Hill.

Rubinstein, M. (1999) *Rubinstein on Derivatives*. RISK Books.

Van Deventer, D. and K. Imai (1997) *Financial Risk Analytics: A Term Structure Model Approach for Banking, Insurance and Investment Management*. Irwin, p. 11.

Chapter

3

··

BASIS TRADING AND THE IMPLIED REPO RATE

In this chapter we look in more detail at some funda-
mentals behind the basis, including the factors that
drive its behaviour, and we also consider implications
of the short future's delivery option. There is also, in
Appendix C at the back of this book, recent delivery
history for the London International Financial Futures
Exchange (*LIFFE*) long gilt future, for illustrative purposes and to observe delivery patterns.

3.1 ANALYSING THE BASIS

Having discussed (in Chapter 2) the theoretical founda-
tion behind futures prices, it is nevertheless the case
that they move out of sync with the no-arbitrage price
and present arbitrage trading opportunities. A review of
the US Treasury or the gilt bond basis relative to the
bond carry would show that the basis has frequently
been greater than the carry, and this would indicate
mis-pricing in the futures contracts.[1] The anomalies in
pricing are due to a number of factors, the principal one
of which is that the short future has the option of
delivery. That is, the short picks which bond to deliver
from the basket, and the time at which it is delivered.
The long future simply accepts the bond that is delivered. It is this inequality that is the option element of
the contract.

We will take a look at this, but first let's consider the
principle behind no-arbitrage delivery.

---

[1] Burghardt *et al.* (1994, p. 27).

3.1.1   No-arbitrage futures price

At the expiration of a futures contract, after the exchange delivery settlement price has been determined, there should be no opportunity for a market participant to generate an arbitrage profit by buying bonds and selling futures; by definition, this is because on the last day of trading there is no uncertainty with regard to the carry costs of the bond to delivery. In fact, certain exchanges arrange it so that the time between the last trading day and date for delivery is identical to the settlement process in the cash market.[2] On the last day, someone buying cash bonds will receive value on the same day, and with the same accrued interest, as a long future being delivered into. Thus, carry cost is no longer an uncertainty and the price of the futures contract in theory must equate that of the cash bond. In other words, the basis is 0 at this point.

Figure 3.1 shows the delivery basket for the 2001 long gilt contract. Now consider Figure 3.2, the same delivery basket for the December 2001 long gilt contract. The bonds have been priced so that they all yield 7%, the notional coupon. Under these conditions, only one futures price will satisfy the no-arbitrage principle. As carry is not an issue on expiry, the no-arbitrage condition is met provided there is a zero basis for one of the deliverable bonds and no negative basis for any of the other bonds. For instance, at a futures price of

---

[2] For instance, the Bund contract on Eurex.

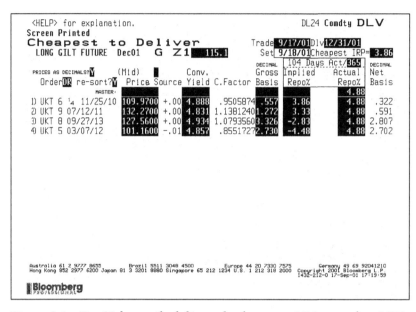

Figure 3.1   Dec01 long gilt delivery basket as at 17 September 2001.

© Bloomberg L.P. Used with permission. Visit *www.bloomberg.com*

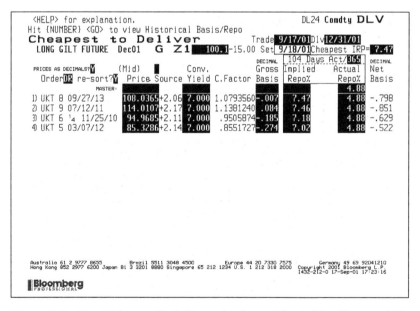

Figure 3.2   Dec01 long gilt delivery basket with yields all set at 7%.

© Bloomberg L.P. Used with permission. Visit *www.bloomberg.com*

100.09, following the price factor conversion the equivalent bond price would be below the market price of the 8% Treasury 2013 – the cheapest-to-deliver (CTD) bond at this level – and thus maintain a positive basis. However, for the 6.25% Treasury 2010 bond, this futures price would be equivalent to a converted bond price of 95.1443. The market price of this bond is lower than this, at 94.9685. In theory, a trader can buy the bond at this price, sell the futures contract at 100.09 and realise a trading gain of 0.1758 (the difference between the two prices). This is the arbitrage profit. So, the initial suggested price for the futures contract is too high. At a price of 100.06 the future no longer presents an opportunity for profit if buying the basis; however, in theory, selling the basis against the 9% 2011 bond still generates profit. The long future must accept delivery of any of the bonds in the basket, however, and will not be delivered this bond. So, the adjusted futures price is too low.

Hence, we know that the arbitrage-free futures price lies between these two levels. In fact, we obtain the no-arbitrage price by dividing the bonds' market prices by their respective conversion factor. These are shown in Table 3.1. The prices in Table 3.1 are the futures prices at which there exists a zero basis for that particular underlying bond. We can determine this relationship easily from the definition of the basis, as shown below:

$$Basis = P_{bond} - (P_{fut} \times CF) \qquad (3.1)$$

$$P_{bond} = Basis + (P_{fut} \times CF) \qquad (3.2)$$

Table 3.1 December 2001 long gilt delivery basket, price at 7% notional yield level, and zero-basis futures price.

Bond	Conversion factor	Price at 7% yield	Price divided by factor
6.25% Treasury 2010	0.950 587 4	94.968 5	99.905 069 22
9% Conversion 2011	1.138 124 0	114.010 7	100.174 234 1
8% Treasury 2013	1.079 356 0	108.036 5	100.089 481 7
5% Treasury 2012	0.855 172 7	85.328 6	99.779 377 9

If we set the basis at 0, we obtain:

$$P_{fut} = \frac{P_{bond}}{CF} \tag{3.3}$$

which illustrates how the deliverable bond price divided by its conversion factor is equal to the zero-basis futures price.

Taking this further, the futures price that would ensure that all the deliverable bonds have a basis that is either 0, or greater than 0, is the lowest possible zero-basis futures price. The price cannot exceed this otherwise there would be an arbitrage opportunity. If we calculate the zero-basis futures price at different yield levels, we will observe that when yields lie above the contract notional coupon, generally the shortest-dated bond carries the lowest zero-basis futures price. If yields lie below the notional coupon, frequently the longest-dated bond carries the lowest zero-basis futures price, and so is the CTD bond. This has been observed empirically by a number of authors, and formalised by

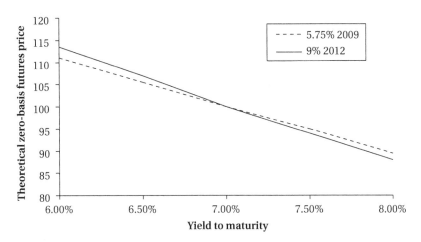

Figure 3.3 Illustrating bias in the conversion factor, June 2000 long gilt future.

Benninga (2001), for instance.[3] The observation reflects a bias in the conversion factor. We illustrate this bias in Figure 3.3, for the shortest-dated and longest-dated deliverable bonds for the June 2000 long gilt future. It shows that the futures price for both bonds meets at the contract notional coupon of 7%, this being known as the *inflection point*. The conversion factor bias determines which bond is the CTD bond, based on yield levels of bonds in the basket and their position relative to the contract notional coupon.

The relative bias of the conversion factor is a function of the duration property of the bonds. For further information on this see Meisner and Labuszewski (1984) and Arak *et al.* (1986).

---

[3] See also Appendix 3.B for a short discussion on a general model of the CTD bond.

3.1.2 Options embedded in bond futures contracts

In the US Treasury bond contract, the short future has the following options with regard to delivery:

- the *wild card* or *time to deliver* option;
- the *quality option.*

The short future may deliver during any business day of the delivery month, although the administrative process involved takes place over 3 days. The first day is the *position day*, the first day on which the short declares an intent to deliver. The first possible day that this can occur is the second-to-last business day before the first day of the delivery month. There is an important advantage to the short future on this day: at 14:00 hours that day the exchange settlement price and, hence, the invoice amount to be received by the short are fixed. However, the short does not have to announce an intent to deliver until 20:00 hours on that day. During the 6 hours after the settlement price, if interest rates rise and the bond price falls, the short will earn the difference between the actual price received for the bond, which is the exchange delivery settlement price (*EDSP*) set at 14:00, and the price that they will have to pay to acquire the bond. Equally, if the bond is in the short's possession, the price received for the short future delivery will be higher than the market price of the bond. The second day is the *notice of intention day*, and during this day the exchange clearing house identifies the short and long parties to each other. The third day is the *delivery*

day; during this day the short future must deliver the
bond to the clearing house. The long future pays the
invoice amount based on the settlement price fixed on
the position day.

The short future has an option of when to exercise the
time to deliver option from the penultimate business
day prior to the start of the delivery month up to the
last business day of the delivery month, known as the
last trading day. At 14:00 hours on that day the final
settlement price is determined, which stays constant to
the end of the month. The short future is left with one
more wild card at this point, known as the *end-of-the-
month* option. Assuming that the short has not declared
an intent to deliver until now, the settlement price for
the contract is now irrevocably fixed. At this point the
short still has five more days before having to declare an
intention. In this case the possibility still exists for
profit generation if, for example, the trader purchases
the bond at the settlement price and holds it to delivery,
earning the accrued interest. This will generate a carry
profit if the bond's running yield is higher than its
specific repo offer rate.

The last option advantage of the short future is the
quality option. This is the option to deliver any of
the bonds within the delivery basket. As we have seen,
the bonds can vary widely in coupon and maturity, and
hence yield, and despite the conversion factor equalisa-
tion there is a bias in this factor that means at yield
levels above the notional coupon, long-dated bonds are
the cheapest, and *vice versa* if yields are below the

notional level. The quality option also presents the long future with potential problems if there is a change in yields sufficient to change the CTD from one bond to another. If this comes as a surprise to the basis trader, it can be potentially very serious.

The delivery options available to the short future carry value, and this is reflected in the difference between the gross basis and the net basis. In theory, the value of the delivery options, when added to the price of the futures contract, should equal the value of the bond together with the carry.

3.2 BOND DELIVERY FACTORS

3.2.1 The cheapest-to-deliver

The deliverable bond is of course the cheapest-to-deliver bond. This is not, as a junior trader once suggested to the author, the bond with the lowest market price (although it might well be). The CTD bond is the one that maximises the return to the arbitrageur engaging in buying the basis – that is, buying the bond and simultaneously selling the future, holding the bond to expiry and then delivering it into the futures contract. Some market practitioners use the implied repo rate (*IRR*) to identify the CTD, while others prefer the net basis method. We assess both now.

Essentially, a good approximation for the CTD is to compare the basis for a bond with its total carry costs to delivery. The difference between the two is the net basis. However, this method may produce incorrect CTD rankings when the net basis values for two bonds are very close. When this happens the net basis for the bond that is actually the cheapest is higher than another bond in the basket, despite the fact that it is the cheapest. This happens because – since the net basis method measures cheapness by comparing net basis to the dirty price of the bond, and this price is related to coupon size, maturity and given yield levels – the actual running cost is sometimes not captured. This can produce a lower net basis for a bond that is not actually the cheapest. For this reason the most accurate method by which to identify the CTD is to pick the bond with the highest implied repo rate. From the previous chapter we saw that the IRR is the hypothetical return achieved by going long the basis and running this position to expiry. It is in effect a repo agreement with the futures market, and the calculation fully accounts for the bond's purchase price. The IRR method is recommended by academic writers because of the way that it is calculated; to reiterate from Chapter 2:

$$IRR = \left[\frac{P_{invoice}}{P_{bond}} - 1\right] \times \left(\frac{M}{n}\right) \qquad (3.4)$$

where $P_{invoice}$ = Invoice price;
$\qquad\quad P_{bond}$ = Cash bond purchase price;
$\qquad\quad M$ = Day base (365 or 360);
$\qquad\quad n$ = Days to delivery.

From (3.4) we see that the bond currently trading at a price that results in the highest ratio of futures invoice price to the purchase price will have the highest IRR. In other words, the bond with the lowest purchase price *relative to its invoice price* is the CTD bond.

Nevertheless, net basis is still popular amongst traders because it identifies the actual loss (when negative) from the basis trade, and as such is a more quantitative measure.

3.2.2   Selecting delivery time

Another advantage of the IRR measure is that it clearly indicates the time that the short future should deliver the bond. Consider Table 3.2 for the December 2000 long gilt contract.

This shows the IRRs for delivery on the first day of the delivery month and the last day of the month. For all of the bonds the IRR for delivery on the last day is higher than that for delivery on the first day. It is apparent that the (theoretical) return from a long basis trade would be higher if the delivery date was delayed to the last possible moment, and so in this case the short future would elect to deliver on the last business day.

In fact, our illustration is a peculiar one, because the gilt yield curve was inverted at this time. In a positively sloped yield curve environment, higher IRRs will result for longer term trades and the decision of the short over when to deliver is an obvious one. The other reason why the short future would prefer to delay delivery is because early delivery eliminates the value of the option element that the short future possesses. It is a bit like early

Table 3.2 Identifying the cheapest-to-deliver and the optimum delivery time, December 2000 long gilt basket.

Bond	Closing day cash price	Conversion factor	Gross basis	Net basis	IRR to first delivery day (%)	IRR to last delivery day (%)	Actual repo rate (%)
5.75% 7 Dec 2009	106.0590	0.917 472 8	0.166	0.300	1.04	6.26	4.52
9% 12 Jul 2011	133.8585	1.147 928 1	0.951	0.509	3.32	2.16	4.52
6.25% 25 Nov 2010	110.8310	0.946 747 8	1.217	1.040	5.79	1.28	4.52
9% 6 Aug 2012	136.2685	1.157 636 8	2.237	1.808	6.78	3.74	4.52
8% 27 Sep 2013	129.9925	1.083 567 6	4.537	4.190	22.70	15.74	4.52

Source: LIFFE, JPMorgan Chase Bank.

exercise of an American option eliminating the option's time value. In a negative yield curve environment the decision is not so clear-cut, although early delivery still removes the short's option advantage. However, the market repo rate would need to be considerably higher than the IRRs to justify early delivery, and this was not the case here. Where the market repo rate is higher, the short future will be running a carry cost each day the basis position is maintained, so this will suggest early delivery.

Even in theory, there should only be 2 days when the short future delivers: the start or end of the delivery month; but changes in the yield curve, a particular bond yield level and market repo rates may make it necessary to deliver on dates in-between. Consider Table 3.3, which shows the delivery pattern for the September 1996 and December 1998 long gilt contract on LIFFE. In September 1996 the gilt yield curve was conventional and positively sloping, and apart from a small handful of deliveries just prior, all deliveries were made on the last eligible day of the month. In December 1998, however, the yield curve was negatively sloping, and this is reflected in the pattern of deliveries. It would appear that some market participants had confused ideas, and although in general bonds were delivered early in the month, some deliveries were still being made right in to the middle of the month. This despite the fact the delivery parties would be experiencing negative carry each day they did not deliver. Essentially, this would have been a cost to all those that did not deliver on the first day.

Table 3.3 Bond delivery patterns for two gilt futures contracts, reflecting the shape of the yield curve at time of delivery.

September 1996			December 1998	
Date	9% 2011	7.75% 2006	Date	9% 2008
2			1	1238
3			2	1787
4			3	26
5			4	4116
6			7	
9			8	200
10			9	
11			10	
12			11	8
13			14	
16			15	
17			16	
18			17	
19			18	3
20			21	
23			22	
24			23	
25	16		24	
26			29	
27	3500	4515	30	
Total	3516	4515		7378

For readers' interest we list the delivery histories from March 1996 long gilt contract through to the June 2001 contract in Appendix C at the back of this book.

3.2.3 Changes in CTD status

A bond may be replaced as CTD if there are changes in relative yield levels of deliverable bonds, if the shape of the yield curve changes or if specific repo rates turn special for certain bonds and not others. Benninga (2001) amongst others has identified the following general rules:

- where the yield level is below the notional coupon level, the bond with the lowest duration will be the CTD. If the yield level is higher than the notional, the bond with the highest duration will be the CTD;
- where bonds have roughly identical durations, the bond with the highest yield will be the CTD.

Bond yields are relative, however, and the bonds in the basket will trade at different yield levels. A large *relative* shift can bring about a change in CTD status, while overall yields remain roughly at the same level. A more significant yield shift or change in the shape of the curve can also have this effect. The yield on any particular bond is market-determined, and is a function of a number of factors, such as its liquidity, benchmark status and so on. If there are two or more bonds in the delivery basket with approximately identical duration values, the bond with the higher yield would have the lower converted price, and therefore would be the CTD bond.

Remember that duration[4] is an approximate measure of the percentage change in the price of a bond for a 1% change in the bond's yield. For a given change in yield,

---

[4] We refer here of course to modified duration, which is usually simply termed 'duration' in the US Treasury market.

then, the prices of bonds of higher duration will change by a greater amount than lower duration bonds. This is worth bearing in mind because it is behind the bias in the conversion factor introduced in Section 3.2.3. Let's reiterate this here. A contract's conversion factors are the approximate prices at which deliverable bonds yield the notional yield level. For the Treasury long bond, then, all conversion factors are approximately neutral at a yield level of 6%. If every bond in the delivery basket was trading at 6% yield, their converted prices (the price at this yield, divided by the relevant conversion factor) should be equal to 100, or close to 100. At this yield level then, the short future is in theory indifferent as to which bond to deliver. However, at yield levels above or below the notional level of 6%, duration of the deliverable bonds becomes relevant.

At yields below 6%, as yields fall the rise in price of a lower duration bond is relatively lower than the price rise of a higher duration bond. Thus, the low-duration bond becomes the CTD bond. As yields rise above 6%, the higher duration bond experiences a smaller fall in price than the lower duration bond, and it becomes the CTD bond.

Appendix 3.A   GENERAL RULES OF THE CTD BOND

Benninga (1997) has suggested some general rules in a non-flat yield curve environment that may be taken to be a general model for basis trading. His study analysed

the character of the CTD bond under four different scenarios, as part of a test of the following circumstances.
When the term structure is flat, the CTD bond is the one
with:

- the highest duration if the market interest rate is
  higher than the notional coupon;
- the lowest duration if the market interest rate is
  lower than the notional coupon.

Benninga suggests that under certain scenarios, notably
when

- the market yield is higher than the notional coupon
  and there are no deliverable bonds with a coupon
  lower than the notional coupon, and when the market
  yield is higher than the notional coupon, and
- there are no deliverable bonds with a coupon higher
  than the notional,

the duration rule does not always apply.

The conclusions of his analysis are that:

- the CTD bond invariably has the highest coupon of
  the deliverable bonds, where the market yield is lower
  than the notional coupon, otherwise it has the lowest
  coupon of the deliverable bonds. The analysis assumes that the bonds possess positive convexity,
  but the results are not dependent on the shape of
  the yield curve;
- when market rates are lower than the notional
  coupon, the maturity of the CTD is the shortest of

all deliverable bonds; again, if the market rate lies above the notional coupon, the CTD bond will have the longest maturity if it also has a coupon greater than the notional coupon. If the coupon of the CTD bond is lower than the notional coupon, Benninga concludes that the CTD will have neither the longest nor the shortest maturity in the delivery basket.

Certain anecdotal observation appears to confirm these generalities.

Appendix 3.B   A GENERAL MODEL OF THE CTD BOND

The price today (or at time 0) of a bond is generally given by (3.5):

$$P = \int_0^T Ce^{-rt}\, dt + 100e^{-rT} \qquad (3.5)$$

where C = Bond cash flow; and
       T = Bond maturity date.

The discount factor at time t for one unit of cash at time $s \geqslant t$ when the time t spot interest rate is r is given by e^{-rt}. The value of the conversion factor for a bond with maturity T and coupon C delivered at time F, the expiry date of the futures contract, is given by (3.6):

$$
\begin{aligned}
CF &= \int_0^{T-F} Ce^{-cs}\, \mathrm{d}s + e^{-c(T-F)} \\
&= \left. \frac{Ce^{-cs}}{-c} \right|_0^{T-F} + e^{-c(T-F)} \\
&= \frac{C(1 - e^{-c(T-F)})}{-c} + e^{-c(T-F)} \qquad (3.6)
\end{aligned}
$$

where c is the notional coupon of the futures contract.

SELECTED BIBLIOGRAPHY

Arak, M., L. Goodman and S. Ross (1986) The cheapest to deliver bond on the Treasury bond futures contract. *Advances in Futures and Options Research* **1**, 49–74.

Benninga, S. (1997 [2001]) *Financial Modeling*. MIT, ch. 18.

Burghardt, G. *et al.* (1994) *The Treasury Bond Basis* (revised edition). Richard D. Irwin.

Kolb, R. (1994) *Understanding Futures Markets*. Kolb Publishing, ch. 9.

Meisner, J. and J. Labuszewski (1984) Treasury bond futures delivery bias. *Journal of Futures Markets*, Winter, 569–572.

Plona, C. (1997) *The European Bond Basis*. McGraw-Hill.

Chapter

4

....

THE FUNDAMENTALS OF BASIS TRADING

In this chapter we consider some further issues of basis trading and look at the impact of repo rates on an individual's trading approach.

4.1 RATES AND SPREAD HISTORY

4.1.1 Net basis history

One of the first considerations for basis traders is the recent (and not so recent) history of the basis. For instance, if the basis is historically high, a strategy might involve selling the basis, in anticipation that the levels will fall back to more 'normal' levels. The trader can sell the basis of the cheapest-to-deliver (*CTD*) bond or another bond in the delivery basket. Let us consider one approach here, tracking the basis of the CTD in an attempt to identify trade opportunities.

By tracking the net basis for the CTD, we are able to see the impact of the delivery option possessed by the short on the level of the basis. Figures 4.1–4.3 illustrate the behaviour of the net basis for the 6.25% 2010 gilt during the period September 2000 to September 2001. This bond was the CTD bond during this period.

Tracking the net basis allows us to observe the value placed by the market on the short future's delivery options. For purposes of illustration we also show the futures price, cash bond price and converted bond price in Figure 4.2 and the actual market repo rate in Figure 4.3 during the same period. The net basis is measured in price decimals, just like the futures and cash price.

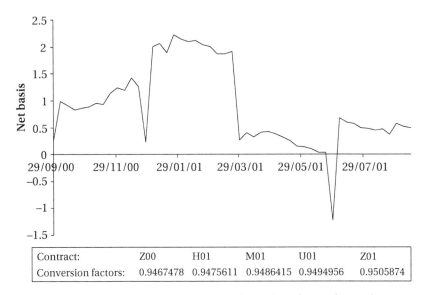

Contract:	Z00	H01	M01	U01	Z01
Conversion factors:	0.9467478	0.9475611	0.9486415	0.9494956	0.9505874

Figure 4.1 Long gilt cheapest-to-deliver bond net basis history, front month contract (CTD bond is 6.25% Treasury 2010).

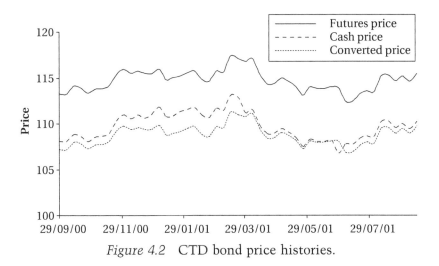

Figure 4.2 CTD bond price histories.

We observe that, as expected, there is a pattern of convergence towards a zero basis as each contract approaches final delivery date. We also observe that profit can be obtained by selling the basis at times

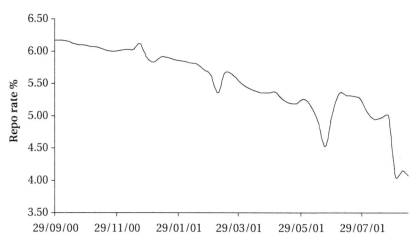

Figure 4.3   Repo rates during September 2000 to September 2001.

approaching the delivery month, assuming that this
bond remains the CTD throughout the period. If there
is any change in the CTD status this will reduce or
eliminate profits, because then instead of the trader
gaining the entire net carry basis, some or all of it will
have been given up. A good way of assessing a position of
being short the basis is to assume one is short of an out-
of-the-money option. The maximum profit is the option
premium, and this is earned gradually over the term of
the trade as the time value of the option decays. In this
case the equivalent to the option premium is the net
basis itself. As the basis converges to 0, and the futures
contract approaches expiry, the net basis is gained.
However, the risk is potentially high – identical to the
trader who has written an option – and potentially
unlimited.

The same approach may be adopted when buying the
basis, observing when it is historically cheap. A long

position in the basis is similar to being long a call option on a bond or a bond future.

An analysis of the net basis history in isolation is not necessarily sufficient to formulate trade decisions, however, because it would not indicate changes in the status of the CTD bond. In itself, it merely tracks the net basis of the bond that is the CTD at that precise moment. A change in the CTD bond can have serious repercussions for the basis trader. A trade idea based on selling the basis of the CTD bond will be successful only if the bond remains the CTD during the term of the trade. So, if a trader sells the basis, with the intention of running the trade to contract delivery, then as long as that bond remains the CTD the entire basis is the theoretical profit. If there is a change in status amongst the deliverable bonds, then this profit may be reduced, wiped out or turned into a loss.

Another approach when looking at the net basis is to buy it when it is historically cheap. This anticipates a rise in the basis value, so it should not be undertaken when the futures contract has a relatively short time to expiry. Remember that a contract ceases to be the *front month* contract[1] fairly immediately once we move into the delivery month; buying the basis when it is cheap is a tactic that is often carried out before a future becomes the front month contract. A long basis

---

[1] Called the *lead contract* in the US market. This is the liquid contract traded under normal circumstances for hedging and simple speculation trading.

position essentially is similar to a long position in an option.[2] So the downside exposure is limited to the net basis at the time the trade is put on, while the potential upside gain is, in theory, unlimited. As with a long option position, a long basis position may be put on to reflect a number of views, and can be bullish or bearish, or may not be directional at all. A long basis trade then is an alternative to buying a call option, put option or what are known as *straddles* or *strangles*.[3]

4.1.2   The implied repo rate

In Chapter 3 we discussed how the implied repo rate (*IRR*) measure was the best indicator of the CTD bond, with this bond having the highest IRR. It is worth bearing in mind that at the start of the delivery cycle the differences in IRRs are fairly small. Identifying one bond at this stage is only a forecast of the eventual

---

[2] As confirmed by Burghardt *et al.* (1994, p. 127), the basis of a bond of high-duration value acts roughly the same as a bond future or a call option on a bond, while the basis of a low-duration bond is similar in behaviour to a put option on a bond. The basis of bonds of neither high nor low duration moves like a straddle or strangle.

[3] A straddle is a combination option position made up of a put option and a call option that have the same characteristics (that is, both options have identical strike prices, time to maturity and the same underlying asset). A long straddle is buying the put and the call option, while a short straddle is selling the put and call options. Straddles require a large shift in price of the underlying to be profitable, but gain in the meantime from a change in the implied volatility (a rise in implied volatility for a long straddle). A strangle is similar to a straddle but is constructed using options with different strike prices. There is a whole library of books one could buy on options, the author recommends David Blake's *Financial Market Analysis* (John Wiley & Sons, 2000), and Jarrow and Turnbull's *Derivative Securities* (South-Western, 1999).

outcome, and indeed it is possible for the CTD at the start of the contract's trading to drop down to third or even fourth cheapest. We noted earlier that traders often prefer the net basis method over the IRR approach; this is because the IRR can also mislead. Remember that the IRR measures the return based on the dirty purchase price and the invoice price. In other words, it is a function of coupon income during the trade term and the cost of making delivery. As the time span to delivery decreases, small changes in the basis have a larger and larger impact on the IRR calculation. The danger of this is that a very small change in a bond's basis, while not altering its cheapest delivery status, can affect quite significantly the bond's IRR.

Figure 4.4 shows the IRR of the CTD bond for the Dec01 long gilt contract. Notice how at the start of trading two bonds were vying for CTD status, and switched positions almost daily, before it settled down as the 6.25% 2010 gilt. This is perhaps good news for the basis trader, as IRR volatility is conducive to a profitable trading environment. More valuable though is the later stability of the contract's CTD status, which lowers the risk for the basis trader.

Figure 4.5 shows the historical pattern for the Sep01 contract, part of page DLV on Bloomberg.

4.2   IMPACT OF THE REPO RATE

Basis trading sounds excellent in theory but market participants also must take into account some practical

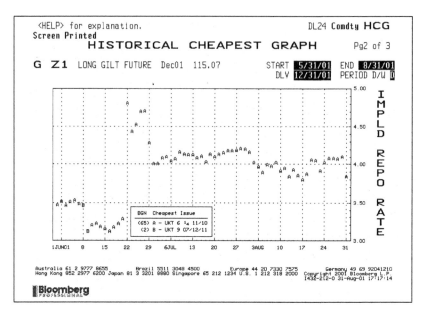

Figure 4.4   The CTD bond and implied repo rate, Bloomberg page
HCG.

© Bloomberg L.P. Used with permission. Visit *www.bloomberg.com*

issues that can complicate matters. Possibly the most
important consideration is that of financing the trade,
and the specific repo rates for the bond concerned. We
consider this here.

4.2.1   The repo rate

A key issue, possibly *the* key issue in a basis trade
involves its financing. From our look at the size of the
net basis, we know that the potential profit in a basis
trade is usually quite small (this being the main reason
that arbitrageurs undertake basis trades in very large
size, $750 million being a not uncommon nominal
value). Financing a trade, whether this is a long bond

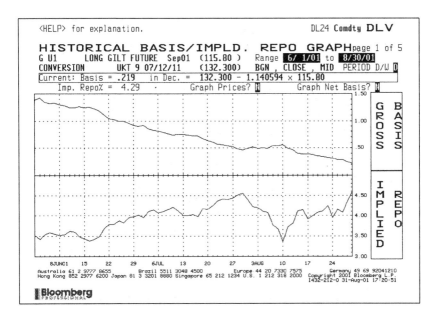

Figure 4.5 The historical basis and implied repo rate, Sep01 long gilt contract.

© Bloomberg L.P. Used with permission. Visit *www.bloomberg.com*

position or investing the proceeds of a short sale, can have a significant impact on its profitability. The trader must decide whether to fix the repo financing for the proposed term of the trade, for part of the term or on an overnight roll basis. The financing rate is the specific repo rate for the bond traded. For virtually all applications, the closer this specific rate is to the *general collateral (GC)* rate the better. In a long bond position the repo rate is paid, so a specific rate that is special will probably render the trade uneconomic. For a short bond position, the repo rate is being received; however, if this is special it would indicate that the bond itself is probably overpriced in the cash market or in danger of being squeezed or made undeliverable, which would introduce complications.

Generally, traders prefer to fix the funding on the trade for a term, either part or the whole term. Financing a basis trade in the overnight does have some advantages, however; for instance, if the short-term yield curve is positively sloping, overnight financing should prove cheaper than a term repo, as long as overnight rates are not volatile. The key advantage though is that if financing overnight, the trade may be unwound with much more ease. In a term repo, the trader is more or less fixed through to his original anticipated maturity date, and under changing circumstances this might be uneconomic. The risk in overnight funding is that a shift in the short-term yield curve can raise overnight rates to painful levels. If long the basis, a rise in the overnight rate will increase the funding cost of the trade and reduce its profitability. If short the basis, a fall in the overnight rate will reduce the (reverse) repo interest on the trade and so reduce profit. In addition, there is the bid–offer spread to consider: someone entering into reverse repo to cover a short bond position receives the repo market-maker's offered rate, which is around 6 basis points lower than the bid rate for GC, but which may be 10–20 basis points lower for a specific repo.

Where one or more of the bonds in the delivery basket is special, it can cloud the identification of the CTD bond. Remember that one method of assessing the CTD is to pick that which has the highest IRR, and if all deliverable bonds are trading close to GC this would be reasonable. However, this may not be the case if a bond is special. To remove confusion, it is better to compare each bond's IRR with its specific term repo rate, and identify the bond that has the biggest difference between its IRR and its specific repo. This bond is the CTD bond.

Uncertainty about specific repo rates can become a motivation behind a basis trade, as it also presents profit opportunities. For example, if an arbitrageur has decided that a short future/long bond basis trade is worthwhile, and their repo desk suggests that this bond may *shortly* become special, overall profitability can be significantly enhanced when the bond is then used as collateral in a repo. Of course, the financing of the long position must be secured first, in a term repo, before it subsequently goes special.

Nonetheless, the issue of financing remains a source of uncertainty in a basis trade and therefore a source of risk. The specific issues are:

- *if long the basis*: for a bond that is currently special, as the bond ceases being special and starts to trade close to GC again, as its specific repo rate rises its net basis will decline;
- *if short the basis*: for a bond that is currently trading close to GC in repo, the risk is that if it starts to trade special, the specific repo rate (reverse repo rate) will fall and therefore the bond's basis will rise.

In either case, this results in a mark-to-market loss. Good market intelligence for the bond forming part of a basis trade, obtained from the repo desk, is essential in the trade.

Trade opportunities can arise based on a bond's status in the repo market. As an example, consider where a bond is trading special in the repo market for term trades but is still available close to GC in the *short dates* – say, overnight to 3 days. In this case the bond's net basis will be a function of the term repo rate, which is special. An arbitrageur can sell the basis, but realise a funding gain by financing the trade in the overnight repo market.[4]

4.2.2 Short bond position squeeze

A market participant running a short position in a bond is always at risk if that bond becomes illiquid and thus unavailable for borrowing either in stock loan or in repo. A basis trader selling the basis is exposed to the same risk. We discussed the issues when a bond goes special in the previous section. The extent of funding loss – when the (reverse) repo rate for a bond in which a trader is running a short goes special – can be very large indeed; there is no limit to the extent of 'specialness' and the repo rate can even go negative. If the bond becomes unavailable for borrowing and so cannot be delivered, it may be difficult to cover and also to buy the bond back and flatten out the position.

In some cases the overall market short in a particular

---

[4] It is rare that a bond that is special to any significant degree would still be available at GC on an overnight basis. The trade sounds good in theory though, although the risk remains that, in financing the trade on an overnight basis, if it then turns special in overnight the trade will suffer. (And so will the trader . . .)

bond issue may exceed the amount of the issue available to trade. This is known as a *short squeeze*. If the CTD bond has a small issue size, it can suffer from a squeeze precisely because arbitrageurs are putting on basis trades in the bond.

To reduce risk of loss from short squeezes, before entering into the trade the arbitrage desk must ensure that:

- the issue size is sufficiently large;
- the stock is available for borrowing in repo and/or the securities-lending market, and is sufficiently liquid such that it should not be a problem to buy back the bond (if a short basis trade);
- both the overnight and the term repo rates are not special – that is, no more than 30–35 basis points below the GC rate. If there are special considerations involved, a specific repo rate that is, say, 50 basis points below the GC does not preclude the trade being undertaken; however, the danger with this is that it is an indication that the stock may trade much more special later.

Once the trade is put on, part of its ongoing monitoring will involve checking that the bond is not about to be squeezed. Indications of this might include:

- a falling specific repo rate, entering into special territory;
- large-size short sales of the bond elsewhere in the market. It is difficult to be aware of this until too late afterwards – a good relationship with one's inter-dealer broker might help here;

- a tightening of the bond's yield against the yield curve – that is, the bond beginning to trade expensive to the curve in the cash market. This is one indication that the bond may be going special in repo.

As part of normal discipline in a relative value trade, there should also be a stop-loss limit, beyond which the trade is unwound.[5] A common approach is to place this limit at half the expected profit on the trade.

4.3   BASIS TRADING MECHANICS

Basis trading or cash-and-carry trading is putting on a combined simultaneous position in a deliverable bond and the bond futures contract. Buying the basis or going long the basis is buying the cash bond and selling the future, while selling the basis is selling the cash bond and buying the future. The trade need not be in the CTD bond, but in any bond that is in the futures delivery basket.

In this section, which is the furthest away from the general area of 'repo markets', we consider some issues in actually trading the basis. It is still of concern to repo market participants though, because the repo desk is always closely involved with basis trading, not least as a source of market intelligence on particular bonds.

---

[5] For an introduction to relative value and yield curve bond trading, see ch. 13 in the author's book *Bond Market Securities* (FT Prentice Hall, 2001), updated in ch. 23 of his book *Fixed Income Markets* (John Wiley & Sons 2004).

4.3.1 Using the conversion factor

A basis trade is the only type of trade that uses the specific bond's conversion factor to calculate the number of futures contracts to put on against the cash position. This is sometimes known as the 'hedge ratio', but this term is not recommended as a hedge ratio in any other type of trade is not carried out using conversion factors.

To calculate how many contracts to use in a basis trade, we use (4.1):

$$Number = \frac{M_{bond}}{M_{fut}} \times CF_{bond} \qquad (4.1)$$

where M_{bond} = Nominal amount of the cash bond;
       M_{fut} = Notional size of one futures contract;
       CF_{bond} = Bond's conversion factor.

So, for the December 2001 long gilt a basis trade in £100 million of the $6\frac{1}{4}\%$ 2010 gilt, which has a conversion factor of 0.950 587, would require:

$$\frac{100{,}000{,}000}{100{,}000} \times 0.950\,587$$

or 951 contracts. The number of contracts is rounded to the nearest integer although traders round up or down depending on their views on market direction.

Conversion factor ratios are used because they determine the bond's basis itself. This means that a trade calculated using a conversion factor ratio should track the basis. In some cases a trade will be constructed using a duration-based hedge ratio, particularly when trading in a bond that is not the current CTD.[6]

4.3.2 Trading profit and loss

The size of the net basis for a bond gives an indication of the expected profit from a basis trade in that bond. Constructing the trade using the conversion factor ratio should ensure that the trade produces a profit (or loss) related to a change in the basis during the trade's term. Such a profit (loss) will occur as a result of changes in the cash bond price that are not matched by movement in the futures price; so, for example, a long basis trade will generate profit if the bond price increases by an amount greater than the converted bond price (futures price

---

[6] It is important to remember that the *only* time when the conversion factor is used to structure a trade is in a basis trade. Hedge ratios for a position of two bonds or bonds and futures should be constructed using modified duration values. The author has come across suggestions that if a hedge is put on using one cash bond against another, and both bonds are deliverable bonds, then the ratio of both bonds' conversion factors can be used to calculate the relative volatility and the amount of the hedging bond required. This is not correct practice. A conversion factor is a function primarily of the bond's coupon, whereas price volatility is influenced more by a bond's term to maturity. They are not therefore substitutes for one another, and hedge ratios should always be calculated using modified duration. To illustrate, consider a bond position that is being hedged using the CTD bond, and assume that the bond to be hedged is a shorter dated high-coupon bond, while the CTD bond is a long-dated low-coupon bond. A ratio of their modified durations would be less than 1, but the ratio of their conversion factors would be higher than 1. This produces two different hedge values for the CTD bond, and the one using conversion factors would not be an accurate reflection of the two bonds' relative price volatility. It is important to remember that conversion factors should not be used to measure bond price volatilities when constructing hedge positions.

multiplied by conversion factor). It also gains if there is a fall in the cash price that is less than the fall in the converted bond price. A short basis trade gains in the opposite case: a rise in cash price less than the converted price or a fall in cash price that is greater than the fall in the converted price.

The other key source of profit or loss is the funding, and this sometimes outweighs the consideration arising from movement in market prices. The long basis trade has a net carry cost, comprised of coupon income minus repo interest, and this is usually positive. The short basis trade has a net carry cost comprised of repo interest minus coupon payments, and this is usually negative. This is sometimes reversed in an inverted yield curve environment. What this means is that the passage of time impacts long and short basis trades in different ways. The long basis will, in most cases, be earning net carry. This will result in profit even if there is no movement in the basis itself, or it may offset losses arising from the latter. The short basis trade will usually be incurring a financing loss, and the movement in the basis must not only be in the right direction but sufficient to offset the ongoing funding loss.

4.4   TIMING THE BASIS TRADE USING THE IRR

4.4.1   The implied repo rate (again)

From the previous section we are aware how trades can be put on that generate profit from movements in the bond basis and possibly also from funding the trade in repo. The key to successful trading is often correct timing, and in this case the correct time to buy or sell the basis. The decision to enter into the trade is based on an analysis of current conditions and historical spreads, together with a combination of past experience, current market view and risk/reward taste of the individual trader. In this section we consider how observing the IRR pattern can assist with market entry timing.

We know that three different values measure the relationship between the current (spot) price of the cash bond and its (implied) price for forward delivery given by the current futures price. These are the gross basis, the gross basis adjusted for net carry or net basis, and the IRR. We also suggested that the net basis was perhaps the preferred measure used in the market to identify the value of the short future's delivery option, and hence also the CTD bond. Figure 4.6 illustrates the three measures for the 9% Treasury 2008, the CTD bond for the long gilt contract from March 1998 through to December 1999. The gross basis and the net basis follow a rough convergence towards 0, while the IRR does not follow such a convergence. The pattern of the IRR also exhibits a certain degree of volatility, apparently uncorrelated to the time to delivery of each contract. The volatility of the IRR has been compared to the implied volatility of an option contract.[7] Plotting the basis against the IRR of the CTD will also show a relationship between the two; generally, a fall in the IRR occurs

---

[7] See, for instance, Plona (1997, p. 290ff).

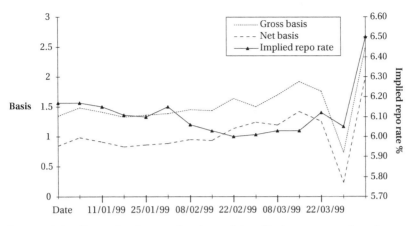

Figure 4.6 Gross basis, net basis and implied repo rate for cheap-est-to-deliver bond (9% Treasury 2008), towards contract delivery.

Source: Bloomberg. Used with permission. Visit *www.bloomberg.com*

simultaneously with a rise in the basis, with peaks and troughs for the one being balanced by the opposite for the other. Further, a peak in the IRR indicates a basis value that is relatively low, while a trough in the IRR suggests a relatively high basis. We say 'relative' because the basis is usually measured across several contracts, and a 'low' basis in March can be 'high' by June. However, the general relationship holds true.

Therefore, the IRR is a most useful measure for the basis trader because it provides an indication of a bond's basis but unrelated to the convergence over time. It also provides 'real' values, not relative ones, as a high IRR is high at any stage of the cycle. Similarly, a 'low' IRR can be viewed as a true low value, irrespective of the time of the year that it is observed, or whether we are approaching a delivery period or not. When we speak of high or low values for the IRR, we mean high or low against the actual market repo rate. Figure 4.7 shows

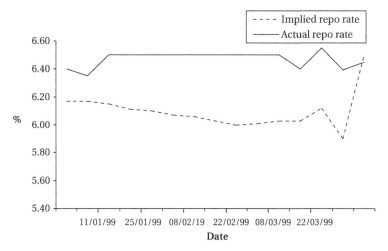

Figure 4.7 The CTD bond implied repo rate and specific market repo rate.

Source: Bloomberg.

the IRR for the 9% 2008 bond shown in Figure 4.6, this time plotted against the specific overnight repo rate (mid-rate) for that bond.

Using the actual repo rate as a benchmark for comparison, we can check when the IRR is indeed at high levels and use this to plan a trade. From visual observation of Figure 4.7 we note that the IRR is almost, but not quite, always within a range that is 80–90% of the overnight repo rate. It is only rarely outside this range, whether approaching the overnight rate or below the bottom part of the range. (Of course, we would be more scientific if undertaking actual analysis preparatory to a trade, and calculate the actual range of the IRR from recorded values rather than just looking at the graph!) Bearing in mind that a high IRR indicates a low gross basis, identifying a high IRR would suggest that the basis has fallen to a lower level than would be 'normal' at this stage of the convergence cycle. In other words, this is a possible point at which to buy the basis. If the analysis is proved correct, the basis will rise over the following days and the trade will produce profit.

4.4.2 The IRR across futures contracts: Bloomberg illustration

The IRR for the CTD can be used in association with the actual repo rates across three contracts on Bloomberg page CBSD. This is illustrated at Figure 4.8, which calculates the swap yield spread at which the long future delivered bond is swapped into a bond that is the *new* CTD and delivered into a short future. Thus, this analysis can be carried out whenever the CTD for one contract is not the same as that for the next contract. The swap spread is user-defined but starts off as the current yield spread between the two bonds. We see from Figure 4.8 that the 'Deliver' bond is the CTD for each contract; the converted price is given as 'Dlvy price'.

The contracts listed under 'LONG' are the long positions in the IRR analysis, while the actual market repo rates are indicated alongside as user-specified rates. These represent the basis trade return (or cash-and-carry return) for the number of days to contract expiry. In other words, the return generated from buying the basis: that is, shorting the future, buying the CTD bond, holding this bond for the number of days shown

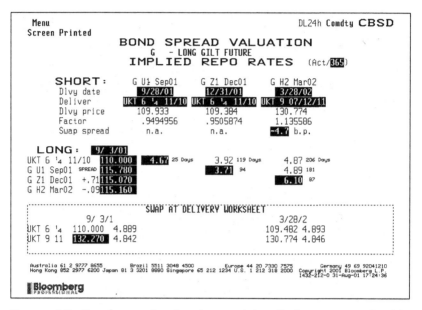

Figure 4.8 Bond spread valuation and implied repo rate, Sep01–
Mar02 long gilt future, 24 August 2001.

© Bloomberg L.P. Used with permission. Visit *www.bloomberg.com*

and then delivering this bond into the short futures
contract on the delivery date.

The IRR indicates the relative richness or cheapness of
the bond to the future, but using page CBSD we identify
whether the near-dated futures contract is cheap relative
to the far-dated contract. This is indicated when the
IRR is relatively low or high, with the former suggesting
that the near contract is expensive compared with the
far contract. Here, then, we are using the IRR as part of
a futures spread strategy. In such a trade, we sell the
far-dated contract and simultaneously purchase the
near-dated contract. On expiration of the front month
contract, the long will be delivered into, with this bond

being held and funded in repo until the second contract expiry. We calculate the funding rate that would allow us to run the position at positive carry using the page as shown in Figure 4.8, from market repo rates.

SELECTED BIBLIOGRAPHY

Blake, D. (2000) *Financial Market Analysis*. John Wiley & Sons.

Burghardt, G. (1994) *The Treasury Bond Basis*. McGraw-Hill.

Choudhry, M. (2001) *Bond Market Securities*. Financial Times/ Prentice Hall.

Jarrow, R. and S. Turnbull (1999) *Derivative Securities*. South-Western.

Plona, C. (1997) *The European Bond Basis*. McGraw-Hill.

Appendix

A

....

REPO FINANCING AND THE CONCEPT OF THE 'SPECIAL'

As we have seen from the foregoing, the financing of a basis trade is a crucial factor in deciding whether to put the trade on. It is important for practitioners to be familiar with the repo market in government bonds and where individual bonds are trading in repo.

The repo market is a vital element of the global capital and money markets. Repo, from 'sale and *repurchase agreement*', is closely linked to other segments of the debt and equity markets. From its use as a financing instrument for market makers to its use in the open market operations of central banks, and its place between the bond markets and the money markets, it integrates the various disparate elements of the marketplace and allows the raising of corporate finance across all sectors.

Repo is an interesting product because although it is a money market product, by dint of the term to maturity of repo trades, the nature of the underlying collateral means that repo dealers must be keenly aware of the bonds that they 'trade' as well. This multi-faceted nature of repo is apparent in the way that banks organise their repo trading. In some banks it is part of the money market or Treasury division, while in other banks it will be within the bond trading area. Equity repo is sometimes a back office activity, as is the longer established stock borrowing desk. However, it is not only commercial and investment banks that engage in repo transactions. Across the world, including financial centres in the Asia–Pacific region, repo is a well-established investment product, utilised by fund managers, hedge funds, corporate treasuries and local authorities. The practicality and simplicity of repo means that it can be taken up even in capital markets that are still at an 'emerging' stage, and by a wide range of participants. It is traded in virtually every country with a debt capital market.

A *repo* is a transaction in which one party sells securities to another, and at the same time and as part of the same transaction commits to repurchase these securities back on a specified date at a specified price. The seller delivers securities and receives cash from the buyer. The cash is supplied at a predetermined rate of interest – *the repo rate* – that remains constant during the term of the trade. On maturity the original seller receives back collateral of equivalent type and quality, and returns the cash plus repo interest. Although legal title to the securities is transferred, the seller retains both the economic benefits and the market risk of owning them. This means that the 'seller' will suffer loss if the market value of the collateral drops during the term of the repo, as they still retain beneficial ownership of the collateral. The 'buyer' in a repo is not affected in profit/loss account terms if the value of the collateral drops.

In effect, what we have described is a secured loan, but one with added flexibility for use in a variety of applications. Market participants enter into classic repo because they wish to invest cash, for which the transaction is deemed to be *cash-driven*, or because they wish to finance the purchase of a bond or equity that they have purchased. Alternatively, they may wish to borrow a stock that they have sold short, which is known as a reverse repo. However, the reverse repo trader is also lending cash. So, the trade might be cash-driven or *stock-driven*. The first and most important thing to state is that repo is a secured loan of cash, and would be categorised as a money market yield instrument.

A.1   CLASSIC REPO

The *classic repo* is the instrument encountered in most markets. The seller in a classic repo is selling or *offering* stock, and therefore receiving cash, whereas the buyer is buying or *bidding* for stock, and consequently paying cash. So if the 1-week repo interest rate is quoted by a market-making bank as '$5\frac{1}{2}$–$5\frac{1}{4}$', this means that the market maker will bid for stock – that is, lend the cash – at 5.50% and offers stock or pays interest on borrowed cash at 5.25%. In some markets the quote is reversed.

There will be two parties to a repo trade: let us say Bank A (the seller of securities) and Bank B (the buyer of securities). On the trade date the two banks enter into an agreement whereby, on a set date, the *value* or *settlement* date Bank A will sell to Bank B a nominal amount of securities in exchange for cash. The price received for the securities is the market price of the stock on the value date. The agreement also demands that on the termination date Bank B will sell identical stock back to Bank A at the previously agreed price; consequently, Bank B will have its cash returned with interest at the agreed repo rate.

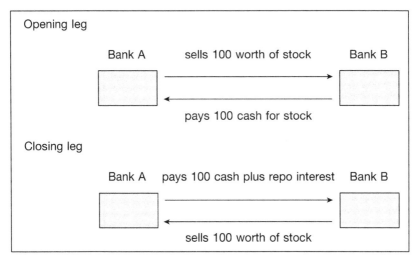

Figure A.1 Classic repo transaction for 100 of collateral stock.

The basic mechanism is illustrated in Figure A.1.

A.2   BASKET REPO: ILLUSTRATION USING MALAYSIAN GOVERNMENT BONDS

Let us assume a securities house buys the current three Malaysian government international bonds that are denominated in US dollars. Table A.1 shows the three bonds and the cashflows associated with financing them. Imagine the securities house, ABC Securities Limited, wishes to fund them using repo. It arranges a basket repo with an investment bank, with the following terms (see top of p. 153):

Table A.1 Portfolio of Malaysian government international bonds, funded using basket repo trade.

Bond	ISIN	Type	Nominal value		Credit rating	Price	Accrued interest	Market value
			USD					
Malaysia FLOAT July 2007	XS0149973850	Sovereign FRN	5,000,000		Baa1/A−	99.98	44,906.00	5,043,906.00
Malaysia 8.75% June 2009	US560904AE46	Sovereign	10,000,000		Baa1/A−	118.44	4,861.00	11,848,921.00
Malaysia July 2001	US560904AF11	Sovereign	10,000,000		Baa1/A−	112.85	287,500.00	11,573,491.00
								28,466,318.00

Source: Bloomberg L.P. Prices as at 28 May 2004.

Trade date	28 May 2004
Value date	3 June 2004
Repo maturity date	30 August 2005
Interest reset	1 month
Wired proceeds	USD 27,043,002.10
Rate	1.33 [1-month Libor fix of 27 7 May 2004 plus 22 bps]
Interest	USD 32,969.93
Maturity proceeds	USD 27,075,972.03

Note that the investment bank that is entering into a basket reverse repo has applied a margin or haircut to each security, depending on what credit rating the security is assigned. The following margin levels can be assumed for haircut levels in this market:

AAA to AA	2.0%
A	3.5%
BBB	5%
Sub-investment grade	10%

The repo is booked as one trade, even though the securities house is repo-ing out three different bonds. It has a 3-month formal term, but its interest rate is reset every month. The first interest period rate is set as 1-month London Inter-Bank Offer Rate (*LIBOR*) plus a spread of 22 basis points, which is 1.33%.

The trade can be 'broken' at that date, or rolled for another month. Table A.2 shows the trade ticket.

During the term of the trade, the market maker will make a margin call at pre-agreed intervals – say,

Table A.2 Basket repo trade ticket, investment bank
market-maker.

Reverse Repo (*RR*)	Contract
Customer ID	123456789 ABC Securities Ltd
Contract amount	$27,043,002.10
Rate (fixed)	1.330 00%
Settle date	03-Jun-04
Lock-up date	06-Jul-04
Total repo principal	$27,043,002.10
Total repo interest	$32,969.93
Due at maturity	$27,075,972.03
Number of pieces	3

weekly or every fortnight. This is done by revaluing the
entire basket and, if the portfolio has declined in value, a
margin call will be made to restore the balance of the
haircut. Table A.3 shows a margin call statement for
1 week after initial value date; we assume the portfolio

Table A.3 Margin call statement.

Fixed income financing margin call	
Date	08-Jun-04
Valuation date	10-Jun-04
Due date	14-Jun-04
Positive number	Amount receivable
Negative number	Amount payable
Exposure	**(27,043,002,10)**
Haircut amount	1,423,315.90
Portfolio revaluation	**(26,593,002.10)**
Margin call	450,000.00

has declined in value and hence a margin payment will need to be made by ABC Securities Limited.

As the trade is conducted under a standard legal agreement, the securities house will be able to substitute bonds out of the basket if it wishes, provided securities of equivalent quality are sent in the place of any bonds taken out of the basket.

A.3 SPECIAL BONDS IN REPO

Specific bond issues that are in demand in the market, perhaps due to short covering required by market makers or because the issue is locked away and not available in the stock loan market, will often go 'special' in the repo market. This means that the repo rate for financing will fall below the normal or *general collateral* (*GC*) repo rate. This acts as the return to the repo seller who is making available the in-demand bond.

In other words, if I am long a bond that has gone special in repo, if I repo out the bond (so my counterparty is entering into reverse repo), the interest rate I pay on the cash I borrow will be below the market interest rate. This is a funding gain that I earn for being in the fortunate position of holding a special bond. Basis traders must be aware of where all deliverable bonds are trading in repo at all times, and also keep a close eye on where specific repo rates (the repo rate for a specific issue that is not necessarily special) may trade in the future, whether above or below the GC rate.

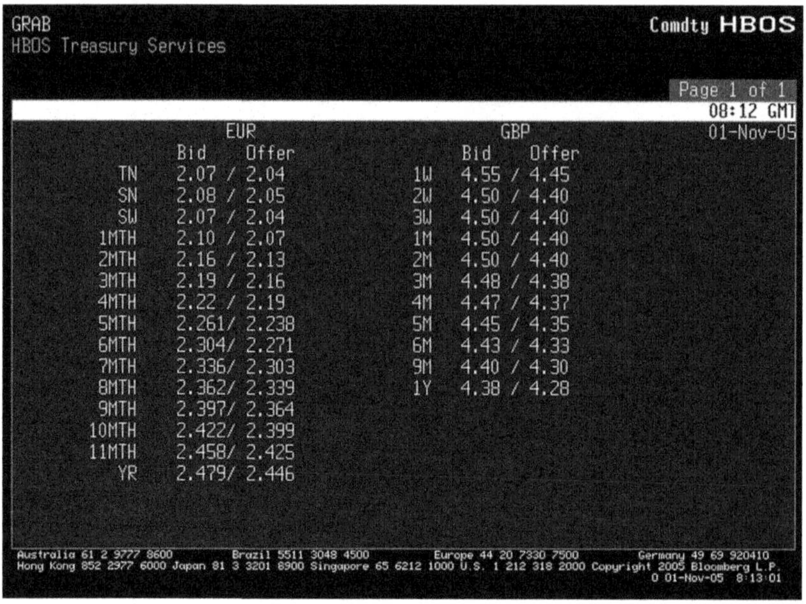

Figure A.2   HBOS gilt repo rates screen, 1 November 2005.

© Bloomberg L.P. Used with permission. Visit *www.bloomberg.com*

Figure A.2 shows the HBOS gilt GC repo rates screen as at 1 November 2005. Figure A.3 shows Bloomberg screen RRRA for the UK gilt 5% 2014. We see that for a repo traded for the term 2 November–16 November 2005 – a 2-week term – the funding rate applicable to this gilt is 4.40%. This is 10 basis points below the same-term GC rate, shown as 4.50% on Figure A.2, indicating that the bond was trading slightly special in repo at this time.

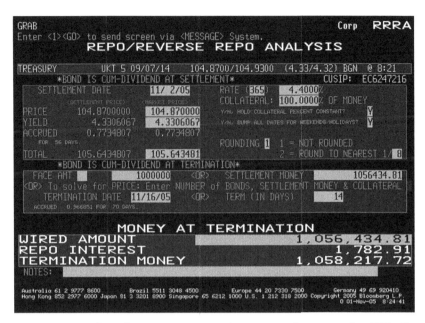

Figure A.3   Bloomberg screen RRRA, repo trade screen for UK gilt 5% 2014, 1 November 2005.

© Bloomberg L.P. Used with permission. Visit *www.bloomberg.com*

Appendix

B

....

RELATIVE VALUE ANALYSIS: BOND SPREADS

Investors measure the perceived market value, or relative value, of a corporate bond by measuring its yield spread relative to a designated benchmark. This is the spread over the benchmark that gives the yield of the corporate bond. A key measure of relative value of a corporate bond is its swap spread. This is the basis point spread over the interest-rate swap curve, and is a measure of the credit risk of the bond. In its simplest form, the swap spread can be measured as the difference between the yield-to-maturity of the bond and the interest rate given by a straight-line interpolation of the swap curve. In practice, traders use the asset–swap spread and the Z-spread as the main measures of relative value. The government bond spread is also used. In addition, now that the market in synthetic corporate credit is well established, using credit derivatives and credit default swaps (CDSs), investors consider the Cash–CDS spread as well, which is known as the *basis.*

The spread that is selected is an indication of the relative value of the bond, and a measure of its credit risk. The greater the perceived risk, the greater the spread should be. This is best illustrated by the credit structure of interest rates, which will (generally) show AAA- and AA-rated bonds trading at the lowest spreads and BBB-, BB- and lower-rated bonds trading at the highest spreads. Bond spreads are the most commonly used indication of the risk–return profile of a bond.

In this section we consider the Treasury spread, asset swap spread, Z-spread and basis.

B.1 SWAP SPREAD AND TREASURY SPREAD

A bond's swap spread is a measure of the credit risk of that bond, relative to the interest-rate swaps market. Because the swaps market is traded by banks, this risk is effectively the interbank market, so the credit risk of the bond over and above bank risk is given by its spread over swaps. This is a simple calculation to make, and is simply the yield of the bond minus the swap rate for the appropriate maturity swap. Figure B.1 shows Bloomberg page IRSB for pounds sterling as at 10 August 2005. This shows the GBP swap curve on the left-hand side. The right-hand side of the screen shows the swap rates' spread over UK gilts. It is the spread over these swap rates that would provide the simplest relative value measure for corporate bonds denominated in GBP. If the bond has an odd maturity – say, 5.5 years – we would interpolate between the 5-year and 6-year swap rates.

The spread over swaps is sometimes called the *I-spread*. It has a simple relationship to swaps and Treasury yields, shown here in the equation for corporate bond yield:

$$Y = I + S + T$$

where Y = Yield on the corporate bond;
               I = I-spread or spread over swap;
               S = Swap spread;
               T = Yield on the Treasury security (or an interpolated yield).

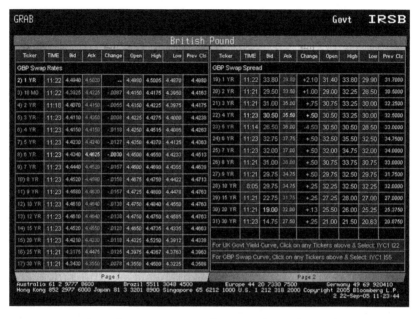

Figure B.1   Bloomberg page IRSB for pounds sterling, showing GBP swap rates and swap spread over UK gilts.

© Bloomberg L.P. Used with permission. Visit *www.bloomberg.com*

In other words, the swap rate itself is given by $T + S$.

The I-spread is sometimes used to compare a cash bond with its equivalent CDS price, but for straightforward relative value analysis is usually dropped in favour of the asset–swap spread, which we look at later in this section.

Of course, the basic relative value measure is the Treasury spread or government bond spread. This is simply the spread of the bond yield over the yield of the appropriate government bond. Again, an interpolated yield may need to be used to obtain the right Treasury rate to use. The bond spread is given by:

$$BS = Y - T$$

Using an interpolated yield is not strictly accurate because yield curves are smooth in shape and so straight-line interpolation will produce slight errors. The method is still commonly used though.

B.2 ASSET–SWAP SPREAD

An asset swap is a package that combines an interest-rate swap with a cash bond, the effect of the combined package being to transform the interest-rate basis of the bond. Typically, a fixed-rate bond will be combined with an interest-rate swap in which the bond holder pays fixed coupon and receives floating coupon. The floating coupon will be a spread over the London Interbank Offer Rate (*LIBOR*) (see Choudhry *et al.*, 2001). This spread is the asset–swap spread and is a function of the credit risk of the bond over and above interbank credit risk.[1] Asset swaps may be transacted at par or at the bond's market price, usually par. This means that the asset–swap value is made up of the difference between the bond's market price and par, as well as the difference between the bond coupon and the swap fixed rate.

---

[1] This is because in the interbank market, two banks transacting an interest-rate swap will be paying/receiving the fixed rate and receiving/paying Libor-flat. See also the author's 'Learning Curve' article on asset swaps available at *www.yieldcurve.com*

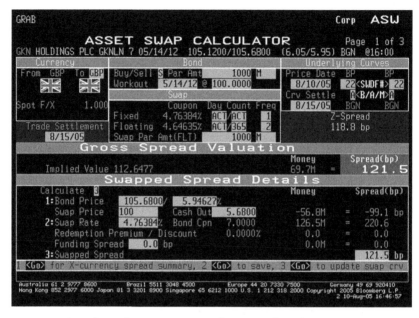

Figure B.2   Bloomberg page ASW for GKN bond, 10 August 2005.
© Bloomberg L.P. Used with permission. Visit *www.bloomberg.com*

The zero-coupon curve is used in the asset–swap valuation. This curve is derived from the swap curve, so it is the implied zero-coupon curve. The asset–swap spread is the spread that equates the difference between the present value of the bond's cashflows, calculated using the swap zero rates, and the market price of the bond. This spread is a function of the bond's market price and yield, its cashflows and the implied zero-coupon interest rates.[2]

Figure B.2 shows the Bloomberg screen ASW for a GBP-denominated bond, GKN Holdings 7% 2012, as at 10 August 2005. We see that the asset–swap spread is

---

[2] Bloomberg refers to this spread as the 'Gross Spread'.

121.5 basis points. This is the spread over Libor that will be received if the bond is purchased in an asset–swap package. In essence, the asset–swap spread measures a difference between the market price of the bond and the value of the bond when cashflows have been valued using zero-coupon rates. The asset–swap spread can therefore be regarded as the coupon of an annuity in the swap market that equals this difference.

B.3   Z-SPREAD

The conventional approach for analysing an asset swap uses the bond's yield-to-maturity (*YTM*) in calculating the spread. The assumptions implicit in the YTM calculation make this spread problematic for relative analysis, so market practitioners use what is termed the 'Z-spread' instead. The Z-spread uses the zero-coupon yield curve to calculate spread, so is a more realistic, and effective, spread to use. The zero-coupon curve used in the calculation is derived from the interest-rate swap curve.

Put simply, the Z-spread is the basis point spread that would need to be added to the implied spot yield curve such that the discounted cashflows of a bond are equal to its present value (its current market price). Each bond cashflow is discounted by the relevant spot rate for its maturity term. How does this differ from the conventional asset–swap spread? Essentially, in its use of zero-coupon rates when assigning a value to a bond. Each cashflow is discounted using its own particular

zero-coupon rate. The price of a bond's price at any time
can be taken to be the market's value of the bond's
cashflows. Using the Z-spread we can quantify what
the swap market thinks of this value; that is, by how
much the conventional spread differs from the Z-spread.
Both spreads can be viewed as the coupon of a swap
market annuity of equivalent credit risk to the bond
being valued.

In practice, the Z-spread, especially for shorter dated
bonds and for better credit-quality bonds, does not differ
greatly from the conventional asset–swap spread. The Z-
spread is usually the higher spread of the two, following
the logic of spot rates, but not always. If it differs greatly,
then the bond can be considered to be mis-priced.

Figure B.3 is the Bloomberg screen YAS for the same
bond shown in Figure B.2, as at the same date. It shows
a number of spreads for the bond. The main spread of
151.00 bps is the spread over the government yield
curve. This is an interpolated spread, as can be seen
lower down the screen, with the appropriate benchmark
bind identified. We see that the asset–swap spread is
121.6 bps, while the Z-spread is 118.8 bps. When undertaking relative value analysis – for instance, if making
comparisons against cash funding rates or the same
company name CDS – it is this lower spread that
should be used.[3]

---

[3] On the date in question the 10-year CDS for this reference entity was
quoted as 96.8 bps, which is a rare example of a negative basis, in this case
of −22 bps.

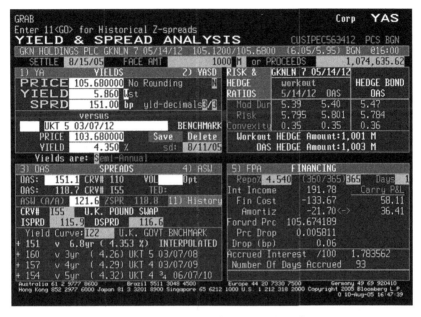

Figure B.3   Bloomberg page YAS for GKN bond, 10 August 2005.

© Bloomberg L.P. Used with permission. Visit *www.bloomberg.com*

The same screen can be used to check spread history. This is shown at Figure B.4, the Z-spread graph for the GKN bond for the 6 months prior to our calculation date.

Z-spread is closely related to the bond price, as shown by equation (B.1):

$$P = \sum_{i=1}^{n} \left[\frac{C_i + M_i}{(1 + ((Z + S_i + T_i)/m))^i} \right]$$ (B.1)

where n = Number of interest periods until maturity;
         P = Bond price;
         C = Coupon;

M = Redemption payment (so bond cashflow is all C plus M);

Z = Z-spread;

m = Frequency of coupon payments.

In effect, this is the standard bond price equation with the discount rate adjusted by whatever the Z-spread is; it is an iterative calculation. The appropriate maturity swap rate is used, which is the essential difference between the I-spread and the Z-spread. This is deemed to be more accurate, because the entire swap curve is taken into account rather than just one point on it. In practice, though, as we have seen in the example above, there is often little difference between the two spreads.

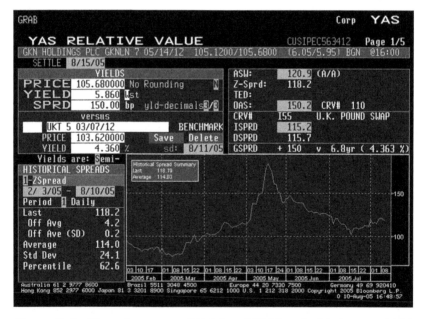

Figure B.4 Bloomberg page YAS for GKN bond, 10 August 2005 showing Z-spread history.

© Bloomberg L.P. Used with permission. Visit *www.bloomberg.com*

To reiterate, then, using the correct Z-spread the sum of the bond's discounted cashflows will be equal to the current price of the bond.

We illustrate the Z-spread calculation at Figure B.5. This is done using a hypothetical bond, the XYZ plc 5% of June 2008, a 3-year bond at the time of the calculation. Market rates for swaps, Treasury and CDSs are also shown. We require the spread over the swaps curve that equates the present values of the cashflows to the current market price. The cashflows are discounted using the appropriate swap rate for each cashflow maturity. With a bond yield of 5.635%, we see that the I-spread is 43.5 basis points, while the Z-spread is 19.4 basis points. In practice, the difference between these two spreads is rarely this large.

For readers' benefit we also show the Excel formula in Figure B.5. This shows how the Z-spread is calculated; for ease of illustration we have assumed that the calculation takes place for value on a coupon date, so that we have precisely an even period to maturity.

B.4   CASH–CDS BASIS

The basis is the difference between a bond's asset–swap spread, or alternatively its Z-spread, and the CDS price for the same bond issuer. So, the basis is given by:

$$B = D - I$$

where D is the CDS price. Where $D - I > 0$ it is a positive basis; the opposite is a negative basis.

	C	D	E	F	G	H	I
Issuer	XYZ plc						
Settlement date	01/06/2005						
Maturity date	01/06/2008						
Coupon	5%						
Price	98.95		YIELD		0.05635		
Par	100		[Cell formula =YIELD(C4,C5,C6,C7,C8,C9,C10)]				
Semi-annual coupon	2		PRICE		98.95000		
act/act	1		[Cell formula =PRICE(C4,C5,C6,C6,C8,C9,C10)]				
Bond yield	5.635%						
Sovereign bond yield	4.880%						
Swap rate	5.200%						
3-year CDS price	28 bps						

Treasury spread
5.635 - 4.88   55 bps

I-spread
5.635 - 5.20   43.5 bps

Z-spread (Z)   19.4 bps   0.00194
The Z-spread is found using iteration

	01/12/2005	01/06/2006	01/12/2006	01/06/2007	01/12/2007	01/06/2008	Sum of PVs
Cash flow date	01/12/2005	01/06/2006	01/12/2006	01/06/2007	01/12/2007	01/06/2008	
Cash flow maturity (years)	0.50	1.00	1.50	2.00	2.50	3.00	
0.5-year swap rate (S)	4.31%	4.84%	4.99%	5.09%	5.18%	5.20%	
Cash flow (CF)	2.50	2.50	2.50	2.50	2.50	102.50	
Discount factor	0.97797598	0.951498751	0.926103469	0.900947692	0.875835752	0.852419659	
(DF Calculation)	$1/(1+(S+Z)/2)^1$	$1/(1+(S+Z)/2)^2$	$1/(1+(S+Z)/2)^3$	$1/(1+(S+Z)/2)^4$	$1/(1+(S+Z)/2)^5$	$1/(1+(S+Z)/2)^6$	
CF present value (PV)	2.445	2.379	2.315	2.252	2.190	87.373	**98.95**

A Z-spread of 19.4 basis points gives us the current bond price so is the correct one
Using this value, the sum of all the discounted cashflows is equal to the market price

CDS Basis
28 - 19.4   8.6 bps
The basis is positive in this example

Figure B.5   Calculating the Z-spread, hypothetical 5% 2008 bond issued by XYZ plc.

Figure B.6 Bloomberg graph using screen G, plot of asset–swap spread and CDS price for GKN bond, April–September 2005.

© Bloomberg L.P. Used with permission. Visit *www.bloomberg.com*

Figure B.6 shows page G on Bloomberg, set up to show the Z-spread and CDS price history for the GKN 2012 bond, for the period March–September 2005. We can select the 'Table' option to obtain the actual values, which can then be used to plot the basis. This is shown at Figure B.7, for the period 22 August to 22 September 2005. Notice how the basis was always negative during August–September; we see from Figure B.6 that earlier in the year the basis had briefly been positive. Changes in the basis give rise to arbitrage opportunities between the cash and synthetic markets. This is discussed in greater detail in Choudhry (2004b).

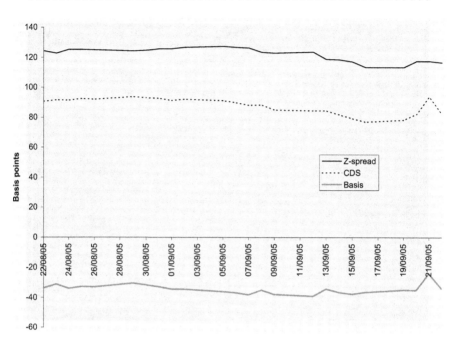

Figure B.7 GKN bond, CDS basis during August–September 2005.
Source: Bloomberg L.P. Used with permission. Visit *www.bloomberg.com*

A wide range of factors drive the basis, which are described in detail in Choudhry (2004a). The existence of a non-zero basis has implications for investment strategy. For instance, when the basis is negative investors may prefer to hold the cash bond, whereas for liquidity, supply or other reasons if the basis is positive the investor may wish to hold the asset synthetically, by selling protection using a CDS. Another approach is to arbitrage between the cash and synthetic markets, in the case of a negative basis by buying the cash bond and shorting it synthetically by buying protection in the CDS market. Investors have a range of spreads to use when performing their relative value analysis.

REFERENCES

Choudhry, M. (2004a) The credit default swap basis: Analysing the relationship between cash and synthetic credit markets. *Journal of Derivatives Use, Trading and Regulation* **10**(1), 8–26.

Choudhry, M. (2004b) *Structured Credit Products: Credit Derivatives and Synthetic Securitisation.* John Wiley & Sons.

Choudhry, M., D. Joannas, R. Pereira, and R. Pienaar (2001) *Capital Market Instruments: Analysis and Valuation.* Financial Times/Prentice Hall.

Appendix

C

···

LIFFE LONG GILT DELIVERY HISTORY

(March 1996 to June 2001)

Table C.1 Long gilt contract delivery notices: delivery month –
March 1996

	Notice day	EDSP	Number of lots to be delivered	Cumulative total
February	28	107-07	0	0
	29	106-28	0	0
March	1	107-17	0	0
	4	108-03	0	0
	5	108-08	0	0
	6	107-30	0	0
	7	107-22	0	0
	8	107-11	0	0
	11	104-20	0	0
	12	105-12	0	0
	13	105-21	0	0
	14	105-23	0	0
	15	105-27	0	0
	18	105-19	0	0
	19	105-22	0	0
	20	105-15	0	0
	21	106-09	0	0
	22	106-05	0	0
	25	105-22	0	0
	26	105-25	0	0
	27 final	**105-29**	0	0
	28		2,359	2,359
Total Mar 96 deliveries			2,359	2,359

Source: LIFFE.

Delivery day is two business days after notice day except on last notice
day when delivery is next day, final delivery day being 28 March 1996.

**Stock delivered
28 March 1996:**   **Treasury 8.5% 16 Jul 2007**   **2,359 lots**

Table C.2 Long gilt contract delivery notices: delivery month –
June 1996

	Notice day	EDSP	Number of lots to be delivered	Cumulative total
May	30	105-21	0	0
	31	105-25	0	0
June	3	105-23	0	0
	4	106-03	0	0
	5	106-13	0	0
	6	106-13	0	0
	7	106-29	0	0
	10	106-10	0	0
	11	105-30	0	0
	12	106-07	0	0
	13	106-08	0	0
	14	106-00	0	0
	17	105-20	0	0
	18	105-24	0	0
	19	106-02	0	0
	20	105-28	0	0
	21	106-06	0	0
	24	106-23	0	0
	25	106-21	0	0
Final EDSP	26	**106-27**	0	0
	28		6,650	6,650
Total Jun 96 deliveries			6,650	6,650

Source: LIFFE.

Delivery day is two business days after notice day except on last notice
day when delivery is next day, final delivery day being 28 June 1996.

**Stock delivered
28 June 1996:**   **Treasury 9.0% 13 Oct 2008**   **6,650 lots**

Table C.3 Long gilt contract delivery notices: delivery month –
September 1996

	Notice day	EDSP	Number of lots to be delivered	Cumulative total
August	29	107-10	0	0
	30	107-06	0	0
September	2	106-31	0	0
	3	106-31	0	0
	4	107-05	0	0
	5	107-05	0	0
	6	106-28	0	0
	9	107-09	0	0
	10	107-15	0	0
	11	107-11	0	0
	12	107-11	0	0
	13	107-21	0	0
	16	108-21	0	0
	17	108-13	0	0
	18	108-09	0	0
	19	108-01	0	0
	20	108-12	0	0
	23	108-00	0	0
	24	108-04	0	0
	25	108-04	16	16
Final EDSP	26	**109-00**	0	0
	27		8,015	8,031
Total Sep 96 deliveries			8,031	8,031

Source: LIFFE.

Delivery day is two business days after notice day except on last notice day when delivery is next day, final delivery day being 27 September 1996.

| **Stock delivered** | **Conversion 9.0% 12 Jul 2011** | **3,500 lots** |
| **28 September 1996:** | **Treasury 7.75% 8 Sep 2006** | **4,531 lots** |

Table C.4 Long gilt contract delivery notices: delivery month –
December 1996

	Notice day	EDSP	Number of lots to be delivered	Cumulative total
November	28	110-26	0	0
	29	111-10	0	0
December	2	112-00	0	0
	3	112-09	0	0
	4	111-11	0	0
	5	111-19	0	0
	6	109-18	0	0
	9	110-02	0	0
	10	110-06	0	0
	11	110-03	1,167	1,167
	12	109-31	0	1,167
	13	109-07	0	1,167
	16	110-04	0	1,167
	17	109-29	0	1,167
	18	109-08	0	1,167
	19	109-16	0	1,167
	20	110-00	0	1,167
	23	110-00	0	1,167
	24	110-18	0	1,167
Final EDSP	27	**110-26**	3,063	4,230
	30		3,063	4,230
Total Dec 96 deliveries			4,230	4,230

Source: LIFFE.

Delivery day is two business days after notice day except on last notice
day when delivery is next day, final delivery day being 30 December 1996.

Stock delivered 13 December 1996:	**Treasury 8.5% 16 Jul 2007**	**1,167 lots**
Stock delivered 30 December 1996:	**Treasury 7.5% 7 Dec 2006**	**3,062 lots**
	Treasury 6.25% 25 Nov 2010	**1 lot**

Table C.5 Long gilt contract delivery notices: delivery month –
March 1997

	Notice day	EDSP	Number of lots to be delivered	Cumulative total
February	27	112-16	0	0
	28	113-05	0	0
March	3	112-14	0	0
	4	112-24		
	5	112-10	0	0
	6	111-31	0	0
	7	111-20	0	0
	10	112-14	0	0
	11	112-20	0	0
	12	112-00	0	0
	13	111-22	0	0
	14	111-16	0	0
	17	111-11	0	0
	18	110-24	0	0
	19	110-03	0	0
	20	109-24	0	0
	21	109-28	0	0
	24	109-20	0	0
	25 final	109-27	0	0
	26		15,424	15,424
Total Mar 97 deliveries			15,424	15,424

Source: LIFFE.

Delivery day is two business days after notice day except on last notice day when delivery is next day, final delivery day being 26 March 1997.

**Stock delivered
26 March 1997:**   **Treasury 8.5% 16 Jul 2007**   **15,424 lots**

Table C.6 Long gilt contract delivery notices: delivery month –
June 1997

	Notice day	EDSP	Number of lots to be delivered	Cumulative total
June	2	112-16	0	0
	3	113-05	0	0
	4	112-31	0	0
	5	113-07	0	0
	6	113-05	0	0
	9	113-06	26,407	26,407
	10	113-25	21,637	48,044
	11	114-03	0	48,044
	12	114-06	0	48,044
	13	114-07	0	48,044
	16	114-32	0	48,044
	17	114-22	0	48,044
	18	114-01	0	48,044
	19	114-01	0	48,044
	20	113-18	0	48,044
	23	113-14	0	48,044
	24	113-16	0	48,044
	25	113-31	0	48,044
	26	114-07	206	48,250
Last trading day	27	**114-07**	792	49,042
	28	114-07	0	49,042
Total Jun 97 deliveries			49,042	49,042

Source: LIFFE.

Delivery day is two business days after notice day except on last notice day when delivery is next day, final delivery day being 30 June 1997.

Stock delivered
June 1997:   **Treasury 9.0% 13 Oct 2008**   **49,042 lots**

Table C.7   Long gilt contract delivery notices: delivery month –
September 1997

	Notice day	EDSP	Number of lots to be delivered	Cumulative total
August	28	114-13	0	0
	29	114-19	0	0
September	1	114-21	0	0
	2	114-28		
	3	115-03	0	0
	4	115-00	0	0
	5	115-10	25,853	25,853
	8	115-18	0	25,853
	9	115-15	0	25,853
	10	115-13	0	25,853
	11	115-15	0	25,853
	12	115-23	0	25,853
			0	25,853
	15	116-04	0	25,853
	16	116-26	0	25,853
	17	117-24	0	25,853
	18	117.27	0	25,853
	19	118-00	200	26,053
	22	118-16	13	26,066
	23	118-07	0	26,066
	24	118-12	0	26,066
	25	118-14	74	26,140
	26 final	**120-06**	58	26,198
	27		1,137	27,335
Total Sep 97 deliveries			27,335	27,335

Source: LIFFE.

Delivery day is two business days after notice day except on last notice day when delivery is next day, final delivery day being 29 September 1997.

**Stock delivered
September 1997:**   **Treasury 7.25% 7 Dec 2007**   **27,335 lots**

Table C.8 Long gilt contract delivery notices: delivery month – December 1997

	Notice day	EDSP	Number of lots to be delivered	Cumulative total
November	27	118-21	1,846	0
	28	118-19	193	2,039
December	1	119-07	312	2,351
	2	119-04	24	2,375
	3	119-08	0	2,375
	4	119-10	406	2,781
	5	118-24	0	0
	8	119-04	0	0
	9	119-13	3,480	6,261
	10	119-22	3	6,264
	11	120-11	0	6,264
	12	121-02	0	6,264
	15	121-02	700	6,964
	16	120-29	6	6,970
	17	120-08	3,887	10,857
	18	120-20	0	10,857
	19	121-01	780	11,637
	22	121-06	3,204	14,841
	23	121-14	0	14,841
	24	121-18	1,210	16,051
	29 final	**121-22**	4,508	20,559
Total Dec 97 deliveries				20559

Source: LIFFE.

Delivery day is two business days after notice day except on last notice day when delivery is next day, final delivery day being 30 December 1997.

Stock delivered
1–31 December 1997:   Treasury 7.25% 7 Dec 2007   **20,559 lots**

Table C.9 Long gilt contract delivery notices: delivery month –
March 1998

	Notice day	EDSP	Number of lots to be delivered	Cumulative total
February	26	123-09	32,898	32,898
	27	122-31	9,753	42,651
March	2	122-26	9,423	52,074
	3	122-24	9,514	61,588
	4	122-09	6,155	67,743
	5	124-12	24,648	92,391
	6	124-06	0	92,391
	9	125-04	0	92,391
	10	125-10	0	92,391
	11	125-15	0	92,391
	12	125-18	0	92,391
	13	125-22	101	92,492
	16	125-30	0	92,492
	17	126-10	0	92,492
	18	126-11	0	92,492
	19	126-04	0	92,492
	20	125-25	0	92,492
	23	126-03	75	92,567
	24	125-29	0	92,567
	25	126-08	0	92,567
	26	126-21	0	92,567
	27	125-24	100	92,667
	28	125-24	192	92,859
Total March 98 deliveries			**92,859**	

Source: LIFFE.

Delivery day is two business days after notice day except on last notice day when delivery is next day, final delivery day being 31 March 1998.

Stock delivered	**Treasury 9% 13 Oct 2008**	**92,391 lots**
1–31 March 1998:	**Conversion factor 0.999 944 2**	
	Treasury 8% 25 Sep 2009	**468 lots**
	Conversion factor 0.929 255 8	

Table C.10 Long gilt contract delivery notices: delivery month –
June 1998

	Notice day	EDSP	Number of lots to be delivered	Cumulative total
May	28	108.96	1,818	1,818
	29	109.15	111	1,929
June	1	109.28	29,002	30,931
	2	109.73	2,254	33,185
	3	109.79	106	33,291
	4	109.64	1,270	34,561
	5	109.08	1,667	36,228
	8	109.19	9	36,237
	9	108.93	125	36,362
	10	109.39	1	36,363
	11	109.94	0	36,363
	12	110.06	3,132	39,495
	15	110.42	99	39,594
	16	109.61	2,201	41,795
	17	108.86	557	42,352
	18	108.25	463	42,815
	19	108.21	0	42,815
	22	108.31	0	42,815
	23	108.30	0	42,815
	24	108.59	550	43,365
	25	108.73	631	43,996
	26	108.08	2,200	46,196
	30	108.08	4,342	50,538
Total June 98 deliveries				**50,538**

Source: LIFFE.

Delivery day is two business days after notice day except on last notice day when delivery is next day, final delivery day being 30 June 1998.

Stock delivered	**9% 13 Oct 2008**	**50,538 lots**
June 1998:	**Conversion factor 1.145 431 7**	

Table C.11 Long gilt contract delivery notices: delivery month –
September 1998

	Notice day	EDSP	Number of lots to be delivered	Cumulative total
August	27	111.62	12,478	12,478
	28	112.33	2,947	15,425
September	1	112.21	457	15,882
	2	111.41	813	16,695
	3	111.90	292	16,987
	4	111.99	0	16,987
	7	112.29	1,402	18,389
	8	112.10	0	18,389
	9	112.49	0	18,389
	10	112.91	0	18,389
	11	113.96	0	18,389
	14	113.41	0	18,389
	15	113.94	0	18,389
	16	113.87	0	18,389
	17	114.47	0	18,389
	18	114.85	0	18,389
	21	115.57	0	18,389
	22	114.85	0	18,389
	23	114.64	0	18,389
	24	114.26	0	18,389
	25	114.97	0	18,389
	28	115.16	0	18,389
	29	115.16	3,421	21,810
Total September 98 deliveries				**21,810**

Source: LIFFE.

Delivery day is two business days after notice day except on last notice day when delivery is next day, final delivery day being 30 September 1998.

| **Stock delivered September 1998:** | **Treasury 9% 13 Oct 2008 Conversion factor 1.142 995 5** | **21,810 lots** |

Table C.12 Long gilt contract delivery notices: delivery month –
December 1998

	Notice day	EDSP	Number of lots to be delivered	Cumulative total
November	27	116.76	600	600
	30	116.81	23	23
December	1	117.30	1,238	1,861
	2	117.17	1,787	3,648
	3	117.71	26	3,674
	4	117.55	4,116	7,790
	7	117.84	0	7,790
	8	117.73	200	7,990
	9			
	10			
	11	117.49	8	7,998
	14			
	15			
	16			
	17			
	18	118.35	3	8,001
	21			
	22			
	23			
	24			
	29			
	30			
Total December 98 deliveries				8,001

Source: LIFFE.

Delivery day is two business days after notice day except on last notice
day when delivery is next day, final delivery day being 30 December 1998.

Stock delivered	**Treasury 9% 13 Oct 2008**	**8,001 lots**
December 1998:	**Conversion factor 1.140 636 1**	

Table C.13 Long gilt contract delivery notices: delivery month –
March 1999

	Notice day	EDSP	Number of lots to be delivered	Cumulative total
February	25	117.17	0	0
	26	115.98	0	0
March	1	115.87	0	0
	2	115.67	0	0
	3	115.96	0	0
	4	114.97	0	0
	5	115.57	0	0
	8	115.8	0	0
	9	115.33	229	229
	10	115.32	0	229
	11	115.82	0	229
	12	115.95	0	229
	15	116.09	0	229
	16	116.32	0	229
	17	117.02	0	229
	18	117.1	0	229
	19	117.22	0	229
	22	116.59	0	229
	23	116.45	0	229
	24	116.74	1	230
	25	116.72	0	230
	26	116.5	231	461
Last trading day	29	116.04	1,110	1,571
Last notice day	30	–	3,482	5,053

Source: LIFFE.

Delivery day is two business days after notice day except on last notice
day when delivery is next day, final delivery day being 31 March 1999.

Stock delivered	**Treasury 7.25% 07 Dec 2007**	**5,053 lots**
March 1999:	**Total**	**5,053 lots**

Table C.14   Long gilt contract delivery notices: delivery month – June 1999

	Notice day	EDSP	Number of lots to be delivered	Cumulative total
May	28	113.98	0	0
June	1	113.63	0	0
	2	112.84	0	0
	3	113.35	0	0
	4	112.92	0	0
	7	112.90	0	0
	8	113.36	0	0
	9	112.87	0	0
	10	112.38	0	0
	11	112.19	0	0
	14	111.92	0	0
	15	112.68	0	0
	16	112.75	0	0
	17	112.95	0	0
	18	113.56	0	0
	21	113.22	0	0
	22	112.08	0	0
	23	111.71	0	0
	24	111.46	0	0
	25	110.36	638	638
Last trading day	28	110.74	3,166	3,804
Last notice day	29	–	3,602	7,406

Source: LIFFE.

Delivery day is two business days after notice day except on last notice day when delivery is next day, final delivery day being 30 June 1999.

Stock delivered June 1999:	Treasury 9.0% 13 Oct 2008	7,406 lots
	Total	7,406 lots

Table C.15 Long gilt contract delivery notices: delivery month –
September 1999

	Notice day	EDSP	Number of lots to be delivered	Cumulative total
August	27	111.15	0	0
	31	110.08	0	0
September	1	110.14	0	0
	2	109.72	0	0
	3	109.16	0	0
	6	109.35	0	0
	7	109.31	0	0
	8	108.50	0	0
	9	107.44	0	0
	10	107.43	0	0
	13	107.04	0	0
	14	107.31	0	0
	15	106.91	0	0
	16	106.88	0	0
	17	107.86	0	0
	20	108.08	0	0
	21	107.29	0	0
	22	107.11	0	0
	23	106.76	0	0
	24	107.71	0	0
	27	107.53	0	0
Last trading day	28	106.8	1,091	1,091
Last notice day	29	106.8	1,914	3,005

Source: LIFFE.

Delivery day is two business days after notice day except on last notice day when delivery is next day, final delivery day being 30 September 1999.

Stock delivered September 1999:	**Treasury 9.0% 13 Oct 2008**	**3,005 lots**

Table C.16   Long gilt contract delivery notices: delivery month –
December 1999

	Notice day	EDSP	Number of lots to be delivered	Cumulative total
November	29	108.39	0	0
	30	108.73	0	0
December	1	108.89	0	0
	2	108.98	0	0
	3	108.42	0	0
	6	108.47	0	0
	7	108.77	73	73
	8	109.73	3	76
	9	109.34	0	76
	10	109.86	0	76
	13	109.94	0	76
	14	110.04	0	76
	15	109.79	0	76
	16	109.58	0	76
	17	108.72	0	76
	20	108.88	519	595
	21	108.81	0	595
	22	108.13	0	595
	23	108.07	0	595
Last trading day	24	108.23	1,399	1,994
Last notice day	29	108.23	3,349	5,343
	30	–		5,343

Source: LIFFE.

Delivery day is two business days after notice day except on last notice
day when delivery is next day, final delivery day being 30 December 1999.

Stock delivered	**Treasury 9.0% 13 Oct 2008**	**5,343 lots**
December 1999:	**Conversion factor 1.130 322 1**	

Table C.17 Long gilt contract delivery notices: delivery month –
March 2000

	Notice day	EDSP	Number of lots to be delivered	Cumulative total
February	28	112.69	0	0
	29	112.65	0	0
March	1	112.31	0	0
	2	112.01	0	0
	3	112.02	0	0
	6	113.16	200	200
	7	113.76	252	452
	8	113.18	1	453
	9	113.81	0	453
	10	114.12	0	453
	13	113.51	0	453
	14	113.39	0	453
	15	113.22	0	453
	16	113.88	0	453
	17	114.74	670	1,123
	20	114.49	0	1123
	21	114.18	0	1123
	22	113.99	1,264	2,387
	23	113.93	0	2,387
	24	113.90	0	2,387
	27	113.15	0	2,387
	28	112.79	296	2,683
Last trading day	29	112.95	1,095	3,778
Last notice day	30	–	2,865	6,643

Source: LIFFE.

Delivery day is two business days after notice day except on last notice
day when delivery is next day, final delivery day being 31 March 2000.

Stock delivered	**Treasury 5.75% Dec 2009**	**5,379 lots**
March 2000:	**Conversion factor 0.912 495 0**	
	Treasury 9.0% Jul 2011	**1,264 lots**
	Conversion factor 1.154 847 1	
Total	**6,643 lots**	

Table C.18 Long gilt contract delivery notices: delivery month –
June 2000

	Notice day	EDSP	Number of lots to be delivered	Cumulative total
May	30	113.41	0	0
	31	113.30	0	0
June	1	113.92	0	0
	2	114.68	0	0
	5	115.20	0	0
	6	114.96	0	0
	7	114.48	0	0
	8	114.60	0	0
	9	114.26	0	0
	12	114.64	0	0
	13	114.50	0	0
	14	114.53	0	0
	15	114.37	0	0
	16	114.49	0	0
	19	114.89	0	0
	20	114.59	0	0
	21	113.82	0	0
	22	113.50	0	0
	23	113.48	0	0
	26	113.05	0	0
	27	113.57	2,291	2,291
Last trading day	28	113.40	0	2,291
Last notice day	29	–	5,068	7,359

Source: LIFFE.

Delivery day is two business days after notice day except on last notice
day when delivery is next day, final delivery day being 30 June 2000.

| **Stock delivered June 2000:** | **Treasury 5.75% Dec 2009** **Conversion factor 0.914 225 5** | **7,359 lots** |

Table C.19 Long gilt contract delivery notices: delivery month –
September 2000

	Notice day	EDSP	Number of lots to be delivered	Cumulative total
August	30	112.45	0	0
	31	112.37	0	0
September	1	112.43	0	0
	4	113.38	0	0
	5	113.12	0	0
	6	112.92	0	0
	7	112.79	0	0
	8	112.80	0	0
	11	112.54	0	0
	12	112.60	0	0
	13	112.01	0	0
	14	112.96	0	0
	15	112.34	0	0
	18	111.75	0	0
	19	112.20	0	0
	20	112.26	0	0
	21	112.44	0	0
	22	112.78	0	0
	25	112.74	0	0
	26	112.45	0	0
Last trading day	27	112.37	0	0
Last notice day	28	–	656	656

Source: LIFFE.

Delivery day is two business days after notice day except on last notice day when delivery is next day, final delivery day being 29 September 2000.

| **Stock delivered September 2000:** | **Treasury 5.75% Dec 2009** **Conversion factor 0.915 704 2** | **656 lots** |

Table C.20   Long gilt contract delivery notices: delivery month –
December 2000.

	Notice day	EDSP	Number of lots to be delivered	Cumulative total
November	29	115.85	0	0
	30	115.69	0	0
December	1	116.12	0	0
	4	116.27	0	0
	5	115.94	0	0
	6	116.08	0	0
	7	116.10	0	0
	8	115.93	0	0
	11	115.48	0	0
	12	115.48	0	0
	13	115.34	0	0
	14	115.52	0	0
	15	115.57	0	0
	18	115.78	0	0
	19	115.53	0	0
	20	115.87	46	46
	21	114.98	0	46
	22	115.30	0	46
Last trading day	27	115.78	36	82
Last notice day	28	–	817	899

Source: LIFFE.

Delivery day is two business days after notice day except on last notice day when delivery is next day, final delivery day being 29 December 2000.

| **Stock delivered December 2000:** | **Treasury 5.75% Dec 2009** **Conversion factor 0.917 472 8** | **899 lots** |

Table C.21   Long gilt contract delivery notices: delivery month –
March 2001

	Notice day	EDSP	Number of lots to be delivered	Cumulative total
February	27	114.91	0	0
	28	115.42	0	0
March	1	115.73	0	0
	2	115.54	0	0
	5	115.55	0	0
	6	115.38	0	0
	7	115.70	0	0
	8	115.57	0	0
	9	115.79	0	0
	12	115.74	0	0
	13	115.65	0	0
	14	116.12	0	0
	15	116.66	0	0
	16	117.11	0	0
	19	117.40	0	0
	20	117.27	0	0
	21	117.43	0	0
	22	117.23	150	150
	23	117.13	4	154
	26	116.97	0	154
	27	116.75	0	154
Last trading day	28	116.25	950	1,104
Last notice day	29	–	2,768	3,872

Source: LIFFE.

Delivery day is two business days after notice day except on last notice
day when delivery is next day, final delivery day being 30 March 2001.

| **Stock delivered** | **Treasury 5.75% Dec 2009** | **3,872 lots** |
| **March 2001:** | **Conversion factor 0.918 980 2** | |

Table C.22 Long gilt contract delivery notices: delivery month –
June 2001

	Notice day	EDSP	Number of lots to be delivered	Cumulative total
May	30	113.23	0	0
	31	113.06	0	0
June	1	113.56	0	0
	4	113.95	0	0
	5	113.70	0	0
	6	114.17	0	0
	7	114.16	0	0
	8	113.73	0	0
	11	114.03	0	0
	12	113.47	0	0
	13	113.19	0	0
	14	113.38	0	0
	15	113.80	0	0
	18	113.95	0	0
	19	113.90	0	0
	20	113.80	0	0
	21	113.48	0	0
	22	113.76	0	0
	25	114.19	0	0
	26	113.86	0	0
Last trading day	27	113.88	0	0
Last notice day	28	–	6,362	6,362

Source: LIFFE.

Delivery day is two business days after notice day except on last notice
day when delivery is next day, final delivery day being 30 June 2000.

Stock delivered	**Treasury 6.25% Nov 2010**	**6,362 lots**
June 2000:	**Conversion factor 0.948 641 5**	

GLOSSARY

· ·

Accrued interest   The proportion of interest or coupon earned on an investment from the previous coupon payment date until the value date.

Accumulated value   The same as **Future value**.

ACT/360   A day/year count convention taking the number of calendar days in a period and a 'year' of 360 days.

ACT/365   A day/year convention taking the number of calendar days in a period and a 'year' of 365 days. Under the ISDA definitions used for interest rate swap documentation, ACT/365 means the same as **ACT/ACT**.

ACT/ACT   A day/year count convention taking the number of calendar days in a period and a year equal to the number of days in the current coupon period, multiplied by the coupon frequency. For an interest rate swap, that part of the interest period falling in a leap year is divided by 366 and the remainder is divided by 365.

Add-on factor   Simplified estimate of the potential future increase in the replacement cost, or market value, of a derivative transaction.

All-in price   *See* **Dirty price**.

Amortising   An amortising principal is one which decreases during the life of a deal, or is repaid in stages during a loan. Amortising an amount over a period of time also means accruing for it *pro rata* over the period. *See* **Bullet**.

Annuity   An investment providing a series of (generally equal) future cash flows.

Appreciation   An increase in the market value of a currency in terms of other currencies.

Arbitrage   The process of buying securities in one country, currency or market, and selling identical securities in another to take advantage of price differences. When this is carried out simultaneously, it is in theory a risk-free transaction. There are many forms of arbitrage transactions. For instance, in the cash market a bank might issue a money market instrument in one money centre and invest the same amount in another centre at a higher rate, such as an issue of 3-month US dollar CDs in the United States at 5.5% and a purchase of 3-month Eurodollar CDs at 5.6%. In the futures market, arbitrage might involve buying 3-month contracts and selling forward 6-month contracts.

Arbitrageur   Someone who undertakes arbitrage trading.

Ask   *See* **Offer**.

Asset   Probable future economic benefit obtained or controlled as a result of past events or transactions. Generally classified as either current or long-term.

Asset & Liability Management (ALM)   The practice of matching the term structure and cash flows of an organisation's asset and liability portfolios to maximise returns and minimise risk.

Asset allocation   Distribution of investment funds within an asset class or across a range of asset classes for the purpose of diversifying risk or adding value to a portfolio.

Asset swap   An interest rate swap or currency swap used in conjunction with an underlying asset such as a bond investment. *See* **Liability swap**.

At-the-money (ATM)   An option is at-the-money if the current value of the underlying is the same as the strike price.

Auction   A method of issue where institutions submit bids to the issuer on a price or yield basis. Auction rules vary considerably across markets.

Backwardation   The situation when a forward or futures price for something is lower than the spot price (the same as forward discount in foreign exchange).

Balance sheet   Statement of the financial position of an enterprise at a specific point in time, giving assets, **liabilities** and stockholders' equity.

Base currency   Exchange rates are quoted in terms of the number of units of one currency (the variable or counter currency) which corresponds to one unit of the other currency (the base currency).

Basis   The underlying cash market price minus the futures price. In the case of a bond futures contract, the futures price must be multiplied by the conversion factor for the cash bond in question.

Basis points   In interest rate quotations, 0.01%.

Basis risk   A form of market risk that arises whenever one kind of risk exposure is hedged with an instrument that behaves in a similar, but not necessarily identical way. For instance, a bank trading desk may use 3-month interest rate futures to hedge its commercial paper or euronote programme. Although eurocurrency rates, to which futures prices respond, are well correlated with commercial paper rates, they do not always move in lock step. If, therefore, commercial paper rates move by 10 basis points but futures prices drop by only 7 basis points, the 3 basis point gap would be the basis risk.

Basis swap   An interest rate swap where both legs are based on floating rate payments.

Basis trade   Buying the basis means selling a futures contract and buying the commodity or instrument underlying the futures contract. Selling the basis is the opposite.

Bearer bond   A bond for which physical possession of the certificate is proof of ownership. The issuer does not know the identity of the bond holder. Traditionally, the bond carries detachable coupons, one for each interest payment date, which are posted to the issuer when payment is due. At maturity the bond is redeemed by sending in the certificate for repayment. These days, bearer bonds are usually settled electronically, and while no register of ownership is kept by the issuer, coupon payments may be made electronically.

Bear spread   A spread position taken with the expectation of a fall in value in the underlying.

Benchmark   A bond whose terms set a standard for the market. The benchmark usually has the greatest liquidity, the highest turnover and is usually the most frequently quoted. It also usually trades expensive to the yield curve, due to higher demand for it amongst institutional investors.

Bid   The price at which a market maker will buy bonds. A tight bid–offer spread is indicative of a liquid and competitive market. The bid rate in a **Repo** is the interest rate at which the dealer will borrow the **Collateral** and lend the cash. *See* **Offer**.

Bid figure   In a foreign exchange quotation, the exchange rate omitting the last two decimal places. For example, when EUR/USD is 1.1910/20, the bid figure is 1.19. *See* **Points**.

Bid–Offer   The two-way price at which a market will buy and sell stock.

Bill   A bill of exchange is a payment order written by one person (the drawer) to another, directing the latter (drawee) to pay a certain amount of money at a future date to a third party. A bill of exchange is a bank draft when drawn on a bank. By accepting the draft, a bank agrees to pay the face value of the obligation if the drawer fails to pay, hence the term banker's acceptance. A Treasury bill is short-term government paper of up to 1 year's maturity, sold at a discount to principal value and redeemed at par.

Black–Scholes   A widely used option pricing formula devised by Fischer Black and Myron Scholes.

Bloomberg   The trading, analytics and news service produced by Bloomberg L.P., also used to refer to the terminal itself.

Bond basis   An interest rate is quoted on a bond basis if it is on an **ACT/365**, **ACT/ACT** or 30/360 basis. In the short term (for accrued interest, for example), these three are different. Over a whole (non-leap) year, however, they all equate to 1. In general, the expression 'bond basis' does not distinguish between them and is calculated as ACT/365. See **Money-market basis**.

Bond-equivalent yield   The yield which would be quoted on a US treasury bond which is trading at par and which has the same economic return and maturity as a given treasury bill.

Bootstrapping   Building up successive zero-coupon yields from a combination of coupon-bearing yields.

Bpv   Basis point value. The price movement due to a 1 basis point change in yield.

Broker-dealers   Members of the London Stock Exchange who may intermediate between customers and market makers; they may also act as principals, transacting business with customers from their own holdings of stock.

Bullet   A loan/deposit has a bullet maturity if the principal is all repaid at maturity. *See* **Amortising**.

Buy/sell-back   Opposite of **Sell/buy-back**.

Cable   The exchange rate for sterling against the US dollar.

Callable bond   A bond which provides the borrower with an option to redeem the issue before the original maturity date. In most cases certain terms are set before the issue, such as the date after which the bond is callable and the price at which the issuer may redeem the bond.

Call option   An option to purchase the commodity or instrument underlying the option. *See* **Put**.

Call price   The price at which the issuer can call in a bond or preferred bond.

Capital market   Long-term market (generally longer than 1 year) for financial instruments. *See* **Money market**.

CBOT   The Chicago Board of Trade, one of the two futures exchanges in Chicago, USA and one of the largest in the world.

CD   *See* **Certificate of deposit**.

Central Gilts Office (*CGO*)   The office of the Bank of England which runs the computer-based settlement system for gilt-edged securities and certain other securities (mostly bulldogs) for which the Bank acts as Registrar.

Certificate of Deposit (*CD*)   A money market instrument of up to 1 year's maturity (although CDs of up to 5 years have been issued) that pays a bullet interest payment on maturity. After issue, CDs can trade freely in the secondary market, the ease of which is a function of the credit quality of the issuer.

CGO reference prices   Daily prices of gilt-edged and other securities held in CGO which are used by CGO in various processes, including revaluing stock loan transactions, calculating total consideration in a repo transaction and **DBV** assembly.

Cheapest to deliver (*CTD*)   In a bond futures contract, the one underlying bond among all those that are deliverable, which is the most price-efficient for the seller to deliver.

Classic repo   Repo is short for 'sale and repurchase agreement' – a simultaneous spot sale and forward purchase of a security, equivalent to borrowing money against a loan of collateral. A reverse repo is the opposite. The terminology is usually applied from the perspective of the repo dealer. For example, when a central bank does repos, it is lending cash (the repo dealer is borrowing cash from the central bank).

Clean deposit   The same as **Time deposit**.

Clean price　The price of a bond excluding accrued coupon. The price quoted in the market for a bond is generally a clean price rather than a **Dirty price**.

Close-out netting　The ability to net a portfolio of contracts with a given counterparty in the event of default.

CMO　Central Moneymarkets Office which settles transactions in Treasury bills and other money market instruments, and provides a depository.

CMTM　Current **mark-to-market** value.

Collateral　Something of value, often of good creditworthiness such as a government bond, given temporarily to a counterparty to enhance a party's creditworthiness. In a **repo**, the collateral is actually sold temporarily by one party to the other rather than merely lodged with it.

Commercial paper　A short-term security issued by a company or bank, generally with a zero coupon.

Competitive bid　A bid for the stock at a price stated by a bidder in an auction. A non-competitive bid is a bid where no price is specified; such bids are allotted at the weighted average price of successful competitive bid prices.

Compound interest　When some interest on an investment is paid before maturity and the investor can reinvest it to earn interest on interest, the interest is said to be compounded. Compounding generally assumes that the reinvestment rate is the same as the original rate. *See* **Simple interest**.

Consideration　The total price paid in a transaction, including taxes, commissions and (for bonds) accrued interest.

Continuous compounding　A mathematical, rather than practical, concept of compound interest where the period of compounding is infinitesimally small.

Contract date　The date on which a transaction is negotiated. *See* **Value date**.

Contract for differences　An OTC derivative contract with a pay-off linked to the difference between two underlying reference prices on expiry.

Conventional gilts (including double-dated)　Gilts on which interest payments and principal repayments are fixed.

Conversion factor　In a bond futures contract, a factor to make each deliverable bond comparable with the contract's notional bond specification. Defined as the price of 1 unit of the deliverable bond required to make its yield equal to the notional coupon. The price paid for a bond on delivery is the futures settlement price times the conversion factor.

Convertible currency A currency that may be freely exchanged for other currencies.

Convexity A measure of the curvature of a bond's price/yield curve $\left(\text{mathematically, } \dfrac{\mathrm{d}^2 P}{\mathrm{d}r^2} \Big/ \text{Dirty price}\right)$.

Cost of carry The net running cost of holding a position (which may be negative) – for example, the cost of borrowing cash to buy a bond less the coupon earned on the bond while holding it.

Coupon The interest payment(s) made by the issuer of security to the holders, based on the coupon rate and the face value.

Cover To cover an exposure is to deal in such a way as to remove the risk – either reversing the position, or hedging it by dealing in an instrument with a similar but opposite risk profile. Also the amount by how much a bond auction is subscribed.

CP *See* **Commercial paper**.

Credit default swap (*CDS*) A bilateral **OTC** contract between two parties who have exchanged credit risk from one party to the other in return for a specified premium. The credit risk is that pertaining to a specified reference asset or reference entity, and on occurrence of a pre-defined credit event the party to whom the credit risk of the reference asset has been transferred will pay the nominal value of the credit default swap contract to the party that has transferred the credit risk. The former party is known as the 'protection seller' and the latter party is known as the 'protection buyer'. On occurrence of the credit event, the contract terminates and the protection seller makes the payment to the protection buyer.

Credit derivatives Financial contracts that involve a potential exchange of payments in which at least one of the cash flows is linked to the performance of a specified underlying credit-sensitive asset or liability.

Credit spread The interest rate spread between two debt issues of similar duration and maturity, reflecting the relative credit-worthiness of the issuers.

Credit swaps   Agreement between two counterparties to exchange disparate cash flows, at least one of which must be tied to the performance of a credit-sensitive asset or to a portfolio or index of such assets. The other cash flow is usually tied to a **Floating rate** index (such as **LIBOR**) or a fixed rate or is linked to another credit-sensitive asset.

CREST   The paperless share settlement system through which trades conducted on the London Stock Exchange can be settled. The system is operated by CRESTCo and was introduced in 1996.

CRND   Commissioners for the Reduction of the National Debt, formally responsible for investment of funds held within the public sector – e.g., National Insurance Fund.

Cross   *See* **Cross-rate**.

Cross-rate   Generally, an exchange rate between two currencies, neither of which is the US dollar. In the American market, spot cross is the exchange rate for US dollars against Canadian dollars in its direct form.

CTD   *See* **Cheapest to deliver**.

Cum dividend   Literally 'with dividend', stock that is traded with interest or dividend accrued included in the price.

Current yield   Bond coupon as a proportion of clean price per 100; does not take principal gain/loss or time value of money into account. *See* **Yield to maturity**, **Simple yield to maturity**.

Day count   The convention used to calculate accrued interest on bonds and interest on cash. For UK gilts the convention changed to **actual/actual** from **actual/365** on 1 November 1998. For cash the convention in sterling markets is **actual/365**.

DBV (delivery by value)   A mechanism whereby a CGO member may borrow from or lend money to another CGO member against overnight gilt collateral. The CGO system automatically selects and delivers securities to a specified aggregate value on the basis of the previous night's CGO reference prices; equivalent securities are returned the following day. The DBV functionality allows the giver and taker of **collateral** to specify the classes of security to include within the DBV. The options are all classes of security held within CGO, including strips and bulldogs; coupon bearing gilts and bulldogs; coupon bearing gilts and strips; only coupon bearing gilts.

Debt Management Office (*DMO*) An executive arm of the UK Treasury, responsible for cash management of the government's borrowing requirement. This includes responsibility for issuing government bonds (gilts), a function previously carried out by the Bank of England. The DMO began operations in April 1998.

Deliverable bond One of the bonds which is eligible to be delivered by the seller of a bond futures contract at the contract's maturity, according to the specifications of that particular contract.

Delivery Transfer of gilts (in settlements) from seller to buyer.

Delivery versus payment (*DVP*) The simultaneous exchange of securities and cash. The assured payment mechanism of the CGO achieves the same protection.

Derivative Strictly, any financial instrument whose value is derived from another, such as a forward foreign exchange rate, a futures contract, an option, an interest rate swap, etc. Forward deals to be settled in full are not always called derivatives, however.

Devaluation An official one-off decrease in the value of a currency in terms of other currencies.

Dirty price The price of a bond including accrued interest. Also known as the **All-in price**.

Discount The amount by which a currency is cheaper, in terms of another currency, for future delivery than for spot, is the forward discount (in general, a reflection of interest rate differentials between two currencies). If an exchange rate is 'at a discount' (without specifying to which of the two currencies this refers), this generally means that the **Variable currency** is at a discount. *See* **Premium**.

Discount house In the UK money market, originally securities houses that dealt directly with the Bank of England in T-bills and bank bills, or discount instruments, hence the name. Most discount houses were taken over by banking groups and the term is not generally used, as the Bank of England now also deals directly with clearing banks and securities houses.

Discount rate The method of market quotation for certain securities (US and UK treasury bills, for example), expressing the return on the security as a proportion of the face value of the security received at maturity – as opposed to a **Yield** which expresses the yield as a proportion of the original investment.

DMO   The UK Debt Management Office.

Duration   A measure of the weighted average life of a bond or other series of cashflows, using the present values of the cashflows as the weights. *See* **Modified duration**.

Duration gap   Measurement of the interest rate exposure of an institution.

Duration weighting   The process of using the modified duration value for bonds to calculate the exact nominal holdings in a spread position. This is necessary because £1 million nominal of a 2-year bond is not equivalent to £1 million of, say, a 5-year bond. The modified duration value of the 5-year bond will be higher, indicating that its 'basis point value' (**Bpv**) will be greater, and that therefore £1 million worth of this bond represents greater sensitivity to a move in interest rates (risk). As another example, consider a fund manager holding £10 million of 5-year bonds. The fund manager wishes to switch into a holding of 2-year bonds with the same overall risk position. The basis point values of the bonds are 0.041 583 and 0.022 898, respectively. The ratio of the bpvs is 0.041 583/0.022 898 = 1.816. The fund manager therefore needs to switch into £10m × 1.816 = £18.160 million of the 2-year bond.

DVP   Delivery versus payment, in which the settlement mechanics of a sale or loan of securities against cash is such that the securities and cash are exchanged against each other simultaneously through the same clearing mechanism and neither can be transferred unless the other is.

Early exercise   The exercise or assignment of an option prior to expiration.

ECU   The European Currency Unit, a basket composed of European Union currencies, now defunct following the introduction of euro currency.

Effective rate   An effective interest rate is the rate which, earned as simple interest over 1 year, gives the same return as interest paid more frequently than once per year and then compounded. *See* **Nominal rate**.

Embedded option Interest rate-sensitive option in debt instrument that affects its redemption. Such instruments include **Mortgage-backed securities** and **Callable bonds**.

Euribor The reference rate for the euro currency, set in Frankfurt.

Euro The name for the domestic currency of the European Monetary Union. Not to be confused with **Eurocurrency**.

Euroclear An international clearing system for **Eurocurrency** and international securities. Euroclear is based in Brussels and managed by Morgan Guaranty Trust Company.

Eurocurrency A currency owned by a non-resident of the country in which the currency is legal tender. Not to be confused with **Euro**.

Euro-issuance The issue of gilts (or other securities) denominated in euros.

Euromarket The international market in which **Eurocurrencies** are traded.

European A European **Option** is one that may be exercised only at **Expiry**.

Exchange controls Regulations restricting the free convertibility of a currency into other currencies.

Exchange rate agreement A contract for differences based on the movement in a forward–forward foreign exchange swap price. Does not take account of the effect of **Spot** rate changes as an FXA does. *See* **SAFE**.

Exchange-traded **Futures** contracts are traded on a futures exchange, as opposed to forward deals which are **OTC**. **Option** contracts are similarly exchange traded rather than OTC.

Ex-dividend (xd) date A bond's record date for the payment of coupons. The coupon payment will be made to the person who is the registered holder of the stock on the xd date. For UK gilts this is 7 working days before the coupon date.

Exercise To exercise an **Option** (by the holder) is to require the other party (the **Writer**) to fulfil the underlying transaction. Exercise price is the same as **Strike** price.

Expected (credit) loss Estimate of the amount a derivatives counterparty is likely to lose as a result of default from a derivatives contract, with a given level of probability. The expected loss of any derivative position can be derived by combining the distributions of credit exposures, rate of recovery and probabilities of default.

Expected rate of recovery *See* **Rate of recovery**.

Expiry An option's expiry is the time after which it can no longer be **Exercised**.

Exposure Risk to market movements.

Exposure profile The path of worst case or expected exposures over time. Different instruments reveal quite differently shaped exposures profiles due to the interaction of the diffusion and amortisation effects.

Extrapolation The process of estimating a price or rate for a particular value date, from other 'known' prices, when the value date required lies outside the period covered by the known prices.

Face value The principal amount of a security generally repaid ('redeemed') all at maturity, but sometimes repaid in stages, on which the **Coupon** amounts are calculated.

Fixing *See* **Libor fixing**.

Floating rate An interest rate set with reference to an external index. Also an instrument paying a floating rate is one where the rate of interest is refixed in line with market conditions at regular intervals such as every 3 or 6 months. In the current market, an exchange rate determined by market forces with no government intervention.

Floating rate gilt Gilt issued with an interest rate adjusted periodically in line with market interbank rates.

Floating rate note **Capital market** instrument on which the rate of interest payable is refixed in line with market conditions at regular intervals (usually 6 months).

Forward rate agreement (*FRA***)** Short-term interest rate hedge. Specifically, a contract between buyer and seller for an agreed interest rate on a notional deposit of a specified maturity on a predetermined future date. No principal is exchanged. At maturity the seller pays the buyer the difference if rates have risen above the agreed level, and *vice versa*.

FRN *See* **Floating rate note**.

FSA The Financial Services Authority, the body responsible for the regulation of investment business, and the supervision of banks and money market institutions in the UK. The FSA took over these duties from nine 'self-regulatory organisations' that had previously carried out this function, including the Securities and Futures Authority (*SFA*), which had been responsible for regulation of professional investment business in the City of London. The FSA commenced its duties in 1998.

Fungible   A financial instrument that is equivalent in value to another, and easily exchanged or substituted. The best example is cash money, as a £10 note has the same value and is directly exchangeable with another £10 note. A bearer bond also has this quality.

Future   A futures contract is a contract to buy or sell securities or other goods at a future date at a predetermined price. Futures contracts are usually standardised and traded on an exchange.

Future exposure   *See* **Potential exposure**.

Future value   The amount of money achieved in the future, including interest, by investing a given amount of money now. *See* **Time value of money**, **Present value**.

Futures contract   A deal to buy or sell some financial instrument or commodity for value on a future date. Unlike a forward deal, futures contracts are traded only on an exchange (rather than **OTC**), have standardised contract sizes and value dates, and are often only **Contract for differences** rather than deliverable.

G7   The 'Group of Seven' countries, the USA, Canada, UK, Germany, France, Italy and Japan.

GDP   Gross domestic product, the value of total output produced within a country's borders.

GEMM   A gilt-edged market maker, a bank or securities house registered with the Bank of England as a market maker in gilts. A GEMM is required to meet certain obligations as part of its function as a registered market maker, including making two-way price quotes at all times in all gilts and taking part in gilt auctions. The Debt Management Office now makes a distinction between conventional gilt GEMMs and index-linked GEMMs, known as IG GEMMs.

General collateral (*GC*)   Securities, which are not 'special', used as collateral against cash borrowing. A repo buyer will accept GC at any time that a specific stock is not quoted as required in the transaction. In the gilts market GC includes **DBVs**.

GIC   Guaranteed investment contract.

Gilt A UK Government sterling-denominated, listed security issued by HM Treasury with initial maturity of over 365 days when issued. The term 'gilt' (or gilt-edged) is a reference to the primary characteristic of gilts as an investment: their security.

Gilt-edged market maker   *See* **GEMM**.

GNP Gross national product, the total monetary value of a country's output, as produced by citizens of that country.

Gross redemption yield   The same as **Yield to maturity**; 'gross' because it does not take tax effects into account.

GRY   *See* **Gross redemption yield**.

Hedge ratio   The ratio of the size of the position it is necessary to take in a particular instrument as a hedge against another, to the size of the position being hedged.

Hedging   Protecting against the risks arising from potential market movements in exchange rates, interest rates or other variables. *See* **Cover**, **Arbitrage**, **Speculation**.

IDB Inter-Dealer Broker; in this context a broker that provides facilities for dealing in bonds between market makers.

IG Index-linked gilt whose coupons and final redemption payment are related to movements in the Retail Price Index (*RPI*).

Immunisation   This is the process by which a bond portfolio is created that has an assured return for a specific time horizon irrespective of changes in interest rates. The mechanism underlying immunisation is a portfolio structure that balances the change in the value of a portfolio at the end of the investment horizon (time period) with the return gained from the reinvestment of cash flows from the portfolio. As such, immunisation requires the portfolio manager to offset interest-rate risk and reinvestment risk.

Implied repo rate (*IRR*)   The break-even interest rate at which it is possible to sell a bond **Futures contract**, buy a **Deliverable bond**, and **Repo** the bond out. *See* **Cash-and-carry**.

Implied volatility   The **Volatility** used by a dealer to calculate an **Option** price; conversely, the volatility implied by the price actually quoted.

Interbank   The market in unsecured lending and trading between banks of roughly similar credit quality.

Interest rate swap   An agreement to exchange a series of cashflows determined in one currency, based on fixed or **Floating** interest payments on an agreed **Notional** principal, for a series of cash flows based in the same currency but on a different interest rate. May be combined with a **Currency swap**.

Intermarket spread A spread involving futures contracts in one market spread against futures contracts in another market.

Internal rate of return The yield necessary to discount a series of cashflows to a **Net present value** (*NPV*) of 0.

Issuer risk Risk to an institution when it holds debt securities issued by another institution.

Iteration The repetitive mathematical process of estimating the answer to a problem, by seeing how well this estimate fits the data, adjusting the estimate appropriately and trying again, until the fit is acceptably close. Used, for example, in calculating a bond's **Yield** from its price.

Junk bonds The common term for high-yield bonds; higher risk, low-rated debt.

Knock-out/in A knock-out (in) **Option** ceases to exist (starts to exist) if the underlying reaches a certain trigger level.

Leverage The ability to control large amounts of an underlying variable for a small initial investment.

Liability Probable future sacrifice of economic benefit due to present obligations to transfer assets or provide services to other entities as a result of past events or transactions. Generally classed as either current or long-term.

LIBID The London Interbank Bid Rate, the rate at which banks will pay for funds in the interbank market.

LIBOR The London Interbank Offer Rate, the lending rate for all major currencies up to 1 year set at 11 : 00 hours each day by the British Bankers Association (*BBA*).

Libor fixing The Libor rate 'fixed' by the BBA at 11 : 00 hours each day, for maturities up to 1 year.

LIFFE The London International Financial Futures and Options Exchange, the largest futures exchange in Europe.

Limean The arithmetic average of **LIBOR** and **LIBID** rates.

Limit up/down **Futures** prices are generally not allowed to change by more than a specified total amount in a specified time, in order to control risk in very volatile conditions. The maximum movements permitted are referred to as limit up and limit down.

Liquidation   Any transaction that closes out or offsets a futures or options position.

Liquidity   A word describing the ease with which one can undertake transactions in a particular market or instrument. A market where there are always ready buyers and sellers willing to transact at competitive prices is regarded as liquid. In banking, the term is also used to describe the requirement that a portion of a bank's assets be held in short-term risk-free instruments, such as government bonds, T-Bills and high-quality **Certificates of Deposit**.

Loan-equivalent amount   Description of derivative exposure which is used to compare the credit risk of derivatives with that of traditional bonds or bank loans.

Lognormal   A variable's **Probability distribution** is lognormal if the logarithm of the variable has a normal distribution.

Lognormal distribution   The assumption that the log of today's interest rate, for example, minus the log of yesterday's rate is normally distributed.

Long   A long position is a surplus of purchases over sales of a given currency or asset, or a situation which naturally gives rise to an organisation benefiting from a strengthening of that currency or asset. To a money market dealer, however, a long position is a surplus of borrowings taken in over money lent out (which gives rise to a benefit if that currency weakens rather than strengthens). *See* **Short**.

LSE   London Stock Exchange.

Macaulay duration   *See* **Duration**.

Mapping   The process whereby a treasury's derivative positions are related to a set of risk 'buckets'.

Margin   Initial margin is **Collateral**, placed by one party with a counterparty at the time of the deal, against the possibility that the market price will move against the first party, thereby leaving the counterparty with a credit risk. Variation margin is a payment or extra collateral transferred subsequently from one party to the other because the market price has moved. Variation margin payment is either, in effect, a settlement of profit/loss (for example, in the case of a **Futures** contract) or the reduction of credit exposure (e.g., in the case of a **Repo**). In gilt repos, variation margin refers to the fluctuation band or threshold within which the existing collateral's value may vary before further cash or collateral needs to be transferred. In a loan, margin is the extra interest above a **Benchmark** (e.g., a margin of 0.5% over LIBOR) required by a lender to compensate for the credit risk of that particular borrower.

Margin call A request following marking-to-market of a **repo** transaction for the initial margin to be reinstated or, where no initial margin has been taken to restore the cash/securities ratio to parity.

Margin default rate *See* **Probability of default**.

Margin transfer The payment of a **Margin call**.

Market comparables Technique for estimating the fair value of an instrument for which no price is quoted by comparing it with the quoted prices of similar instruments.

Market maker Market participant who is committed, explicitly or otherwise, to quoting two-way bid and offer prices at all times in a particular market.

Market risk Risks related to changes in prices of tradeable macro-economic variables, such as exchange rate risks.

Mark-to-market The act of revaluing securities to current market values. Such revaluations should include both coupon accrued on the securities outstanding and interest accrued on the cash.

Matched book This refers to the matching by a **repo** trader of securities repoed in and out. It carries no implications that the trader's position is 'matched' in terms of exposure – for example, to short-term interest rates.

Maturity date Date on which stock is redeemed.

Mean Average.

Modified following The convention that if a value date in the future falls on a non-business day, the value date will be moved to the next following business day, unless this moves the value date to the next month, in which case the value date is moved back to the last previous business day.

Money market Short-term market (generally up to 1 year) for financial instruments. *See* **Capital market**.

Money-market basis An interest rate quoted on an **ACT/360** basis is said to be on a money-market basis. *See* **Bond basis**.

Monte Carlo simulation Technique used to determine the likely value of a derivative or other contract by simulating the evolution of the underlying variables many times. The discounted average outcome of the simulation gives an approximation of the derivative's value. Monte Carlo simulation can be used to estimate the **Value-at-risk (VAR)** of a portfolio. Here, it generates a simulation of many correlated market movements for the markets to which the portfolio is exposed, and the positions in the portfolio are revalued repeatedly in accordance with the simulated scenarios. This gives a probability distribution of portfolio gains and losses from which the VAR can be determined.

Moosmuller   A method for calculating the yield of a bond.

Mortgage-backed security (MBS)   Security guaranteed by a pool of mortgages. MBS markets include the US, UK, Japan and Denmark.

Moving average convergence/divergence (MACD)   The crossing of two exponentially smoothed moving averages that oscillate above and below an equilibrium line.

Naked   A naked **Option** position is one not protected by an offsetting position in the **Underlying**. *See* **Covered call/put**.

Negative divergence   When at least two indicators, indexes or averages show conflicting or contradictory trends.

Negotiable   A security which can be bought and sold in a **Secondary market** is negotiable.

Net present value (NPV)   The net present value of a series of cash flows is the sum of the present values of each cash flow (some or all of which may be negative).

Noise   Fluctuations in the market which can confuse or impede interpretation of market direction.

Nominal amount   Same as **Face value** of a security.

Nominal rate   A rate of interest as quoted, rather than the **Effective rate** to which it is equivalent.

Normal   A normal **Probability distribution** is a particular distribution assumed to prevail in a wide variety of circumstances, including the financial markets. Mathematically, it corresponds to the probability density function $\dfrac{1}{\sqrt{2\pi}}e^{-\frac{1}{2}\phi^2}$.

Notional   In a bond futures contract, the bond bought or sold is a standardised non-existent notional bond, as opposed to the actual bonds which are **Deliverable** at maturity. **Contracts for differ-**

ences also require a notional principal amount on which settlement can be calculated.

Novation   Replacement of a contract or, more usually, a series of contracts with one new contract.

NPV   *See* **Net present value.**

O/N   *See* **Overnight.**

Odd date   *See* **Broken date.**

Offer   The price at which a market maker will sell bonds. Also called 'ask'.

Off-market   A rate which is not the current market rate.

Opening leg   The first half of a **repo** transaction.

Open interest   The quantity of **Futures** contracts (of a particular specification) which have not yet been closed out by reversing. Either all **Long** positions or all **Short** positions are counted but not both.

Operational Market Notice   Sets out the DMO's (previously the Bank's) operations and procedures in the gilt market.

Operational risk   Risk of loss occurring due to inadequate systems and control, human error or management failure.

Opportunity cost   Value of an action that could have been taken if the current action had not been chosen.

Option   The right (but not the obligation) to buy or sell securities at a fixed price within a specified period.

Option forward   *See* **Time option.**

OTC (over the counter)   Strictly speaking, any transaction not conducted on a registered stock exchange. Trades conducted via the telephone between banks, and contracts such as FRAs and (non-exchange-traded) options are said to be 'over-the-counter' instruments. OTC also refers to non-standard instruments or contracts traded between two parties – for example, a client with a requirement for a specific risk to be hedged with a tailor-made instrument may enter into an OTC structured option trade with a bank that makes markets in such products.

Over the counter   An OTC transaction is one dealt privately between any two parties, with all details agreed between them, as opposed to one dealt on an exchange – for example, a **Forward** deal as opposed to a **Futures contract.**

Overborrowed   A position in which a dealer's liabilities (borrowings taken in) are of longer maturity than the assets (loans out).

Overlent   A position in which a dealer's assets (loans out) are of longer maturity than the liabilities (borrowings taken in).

Overnight (*O/N*)   A deal from today until the next working day ('tomorrow').

Paper   Another term for a bond or debt issue.

Par   In foreign exchange, when the outright and **Spot** exchange rates are equal, the **Forward swap** is 0 or par. When the price of a security is equal to the face value, usually expressed as 100, it is said to be trading at par. A par swap rate is the current market rate for a fixed **Interest rate swap** against **LIBOR**.

Par yield curve   A curve plotting maturity against **Yield** for bonds priced at par.

Parity   The official rate of exchange for one currency in terms of another which a government is obliged to maintain by means of intervention.

Pips   *See* **Points**.

Plain vanilla   *See* **Vanilla**.

Points   The last two decimal places in an exchange rate. For example, when EUR/USD is 1.1910/1.1920, the points are 10/20. *See* **Bid figure**.

Premium   The forward premium is the amount by which a currency is more expensive, in terms of another currency, for future delivery than for spot (in general, a reflection of interest rate differentials between two currencies). If an exchange rate is 'at a premium' (without specifying to which of the two currencies this refers), this generally means that the **Variable currency** is at a premium. *See* **Discount**.

Present value   The amount of money which needs to be invested now to achieve a given amount in the future when interest is added. *See* **Time value of money**, **Future value**.

Pre-settlement risk   As distinct from credit risk arising from intraday settlement risk, this term describes the risk of loss that might be suffered during the life of the contract if a counterparty to a trade defaulted and if, at the time of the default, the instrument had a positive economic value.

Price–earnings ratio   A ratio giving the price of a stock relative to the earnings per share.

Price factor   *See* **Conversion factor**.

Primary market The market for new debt, into which new bonds are issued. The primary market is made up of borrowers, investors and the investment banks which place new debt into the market, usually with their clients. Bonds that trade after they have been issued are said to be part of the secondary market.

Probability distribution The mathematical description of how probable it is that the value of something is less than or equal to a particular level.

Put A put option is an option to sell the commodity or instrument **Underlying** the option. *See* **Call**.

Quanto An option that has its final payoff linked to two or more underlying assets or reference rates.

Quanto swap A **Swap** where the payments of one or both legs are based on a measurement (such as the interest rate) in one currency but payable in another currency.

Quasi-coupon date The regular date for which a **Coupon** payment would be scheduled if there were one. Used for price/yield calculations for **Zero-coupon** instruments.

Record date A **Coupon** or other payment due on a security is paid by the issuer to whoever is registered on the record date as being the owner. *See* **Ex-dividend**, **Cum dividend**.

Redeem A security is said to be redeemed when the principal is repaid.

Redemption yield The rate of interest at which all future payments (coupons and redemption) on a bond are discounted so that their total equals the current price of the bond (inversely related to price).

Redenomination A change in the currency unit in which the nominal value of a security is expressed (in context, from sterling to euro).

Refer The practice whereby a trader instructs a broker to put 'under reference' any prices or rates he has quoted to him, meaning that they are no longer 'firm' and the broker must refer to the trader before he can trade on the price initially quoted.

Register Record of ownership of securities. For gilts, excluding bearer bonds, entry in an official register confers title.

Registered bond A bond for which the issuer keeps a record (register) of its owners. Transfer of ownership must be notified and recorded in the register. Interest payments are posted (more usually electronically transferred) to the bond holder.

Registrar's department Department of the Bank of England which maintains the register of holdings of gilts.

Reinvestment rate The rate at which interest paid during the life of an investment is reinvested to earn interest-on-interest, which in practice will generally not be the same as the original yield quoted on the investment.

Repo Usually refers in particular to **Classic repo**. Also used as a term to include **Buy/sell-backs** and **Securities lending**.

Repo rate The return earned on a repo transaction expressed as an interest rate on the cash side of the transaction.

Repurchase agreement *See* **Repo**.

Return on assets The net earnings of a company divided by its assets.

Return on equity The net earnings of a company divided by its equity.

Reverse *See* **Reverse repo**.

Reverse repo The opposite of a **Repo**.

Rollover *See* **Tom/next**. Also refers to a renewal of a loan.

Rump A gilt issue so designated because it is illiquid, generally because there is a very small nominal amount left in existence.

Running yield Same as **Current yield**.

S/N *See* **Spot/next**.

SAFE *See* **Synthetic** agreement for forward exchange.

Secondary market The market in instruments after they have been issued. Bonds are bought and sold after their initial issue by the borrower, and the marketplace for this buying and selling is referred to as the 'secondary market'. The new issues market is the primary market.

Securities lending When a specific security is lent against some form of **Collateral**. Also known as 'stock lending'.

Security A financial asset sold initially for cash by a borrowing organisation (the 'issuer'). The security is often negotiable and usually has a maturity date when it is redeemed.

Sell/buy-back Simultaneous spot sale and forward purchase of a security, with the forward price calculated to achieve an effect equivalent to a **Classic repo**.

Settlement The process of transferring stock from seller to buyer and arranging the corresponding movement of funds between the two parties.

Settlement bank Bank which agrees to receive and make assured payments for gilts bought and sold by a CGO member.

Settlement date Date on which transfers of gilts and payment occur, usually the next working day after the trade is conducted.

Settlement risk This occurs when there is a non-simultaneous exchange of value. Also known as 'delivery risk' and 'Herstatt risk'.

Short A short position is a surplus of sales over purchases of a given currency or asset, or a situation which naturally gives rise to an organisation benefiting from a weakening of that currency or asset. To a money market dealer, however, a short position is a surplus of money lent out over borrowings taken in (which give rise to a benefit if that currency strengthens rather than weakens). *See* **Long**.

Short date A deal for value on a date other than **Spot** but less than 1 month after spot.

Simple interest When interest on an investment is paid all at maturity or not reinvested to earn interest on interest, the interest is said to be simple. *See* **Compound interest**.

Simple yield to maturity Bond coupon plus principal gain/loss amortised over the time to maturity, as a proportion of the clean price per 100. Does not take **Time value of money** into account. *See* **Yield to maturity**, **Current yield**.

Special A security which for any reason is sought after in the **Repo** market, thereby enabling any holder of the security to earn incremental income (in excess of the **General collateral** rate) through lending them via a repo transaction. The repo rate for a special will be below the GC rate, as this is the rate the borrower of the cash is paying in return for supplying the special bond as **Collateral**. An individual security can be in high demand for a variety of reasons – for instance, if there is sudden heavy investor demand for it, or (if it is a benchmark issue), it is required as a hedge against a new issue of similar maturity paper.

Speculation A deal undertaken because the dealer expects prices to move in their favour, as opposed to **Hedging** or **Arbitrage**.

Spot A deal to be settled on the customary value date for that particular market. In the foreign exchange market, this is for value in 2 working days' time.

Spot/next A transaction from **Spot** until the next working day.

Spread The difference between the bid and offer prices in a quotation. Also a strategy involving the purchase of an instrument and the simultaneous sale of a similar related instrument, such as the purchase of a **Call option** at one **Strike** and the sale of a call option at a different strike.

Square A position in which sales exactly match purchases, or in which assets exactly match liabilities. *See* **Long**, **Short**.

Standard deviation (*E*) A measure of how much the values of something fluctuate around its mean value. Defined as the square root of the **Variance**.

Stock lending *See* **Securities lending.**

Stock index future Future on a stock index, allowing a hedge against, or bet on, a broad equity market movement.

Stock index option Option on a stock index future.

Stock option Option on an individual stock.

Street The 'street' is a term for the market, originating as 'Wall Street'. A US term for market convention, so in the US market is the convention for quoting the price or yield for a particular instrument.

Strike The strike price or strike rate of an option is the price or rate at which the holder can insist on the underlying transaction being fulfilled.

Strip A **Zero-coupon bond** which is produced by separating a standard coupon-bearing bond into its constituent principal and interest components. To strip a bond is to separate its principal amount and its coupons and trade each individual cashflow as a separate instrument ('separately traded and registered for interest and principal'). Also, a strip of **Futures** is a series of short-term futures contracts with consecutive delivery dates, which together create the effect of a longer term instrument (for example, four consecutive 3-month futures contracts as a **Hedge** against a 1-year swap). A strip of **FRAs** is similar.

Swap A foreign exchange swap is the purchase of one currency against another for delivery on one date, with a simultaneous sale to reverse the transaction on another value date. *See also* **Interest rate swap**, **Currency swap**.

Swaption An **Option** on an **Interest rate swap**, **Currency swap**.

Switch Exchanges of one gilt holding for another, sometimes entered into between the DMO and a GEMM as part of the DMO's secondary market operations.

Synthetic A package of transactions which is economically equivalent to a different transaction (for example, the purchase of a **Call option** and simultaneous sale of a **Put** option at the same **Strike** is a synthetic **Forward** purchase).

T/N *See* **Tom/next**.

Tail The exposure to interest rates over a forward–forward period arising from a mismatched position (such as a 2-month borrowing against a 3-month loan). A forward foreign exchange dealer's exposure to **Spot** movements.

Tap The issue of a gilt for exceptional market management reasons and not on a pre-announced schedule.

Term The time between the beginning and end of a deal or investment.

Tick The minimum change allowed in a **Futures** price.

Time deposit A non-**Negotiable** deposit for a specific term.

Time option A forward currency deal in which the value date is set to be within a period rather than on a particular day. The customer sets the exact date 2 working days before settlement.

Time value of money The concept that a future cashflow can be valued as the amount of money which it is necessary to invest now in order to achieve that cashflow in the future. *See* **Present value**, **Future value**.

Today/tomorrow *See* **Overnight**.

Tom/next A transaction from the next working day ('tomorrow') until the day after ('next day' – i.e., **Spot** in the foreign exchange market).

Total return swap Swap agreement in which the total return of bank loans or credit-sensitive securities is exchanged for some other cash flow usually tied to **LIBOR**, or other loans, or credit-sensitive securities. It allows participants to effectively go **Long** or **Short** the credit risk of the **Underlying** asset.

Traded option Option that is listed on and cleared by an exchange, with standard terms and delivery months.

Tranche One of a series of two or more issues with the same coupon rate and maturity date. The tranches become **Fungible** at a future date, usually just after the first coupon date.

Transaction risk Extent to which the value of transactions that have already been agreed is affected by market risk.

Transparent A term used to refer to how clear asset prices are in a market. A transparent market is one in which a majority of market participants are aware of what level a particular bond or instrument is trading.

Treasury bill A short-term security issued by a government, generally with a **Zero-coupon.**

Uncovered option When the **Writer** of the option does not own the **Underlying** security. Also known as a **Naked** option.

Undated gilts Gilts for which there is no final date by which the gilt must be redeemed.

Underlying The underlying of a **Futures** or option contract is the commodity or financial instrument on which the contract depends. Thus, the underlying for a bond option is the bond; the underlying for a short-term interest rate futures contract is typically a 3-month deposit.

Underwriting An arrangement by which a company is guaranteed that an issue of debt (bonds) will raise a given amount of cash. Underwriting is carried out by investment banks, who undertake to purchase any part of the debt issue not taken up by the public. A commission is charged for this service.

Value-at-risk (*VAR*) Formally, the probabilistic bound of market losses over a given period of time (known as the 'holding period') expressed in terms of a specified degree of certainty (known as the 'confidence interval'). Put more simply, the VAR is the worst case loss that would be expected over the holding period within the probability set out by the confidence interval. Larger losses are possible but with a low probability. For instance, a portfolio whose VAR is $20 million over a 1-day holding period, with a 95% confidence interval, would have only a 5% chance of suffering an overnight loss greater than $20 million.

Value date The date on which a deal is to be consummated. In some bond markets, the value date for coupon accruals can sometimes differ from the settlement date.

Vanilla A vanilla transaction is a straightforward one.

VAR *See* **Value-at-risk**.

Variable currency Exchange rates are quoted in terms of the number of units of one currency (the variable or counter currency) which corresponds to 1 unit of the other currency (the **Base currency**).

Variance (E^2) A measure of how much the values of something fluctuate around its mean value. Defined as the average of (Value − Mean)^2. *See* **Standard deviation**.

Variance–covariance methodology Methodology for calculating the **Value-at-risk** of a portfolio as a function of the **Volatility** of each asset or liability position in the portfolio and the correlation between the positions.

Variation margin The band agreed between the parties to a **Repo** transaction at the outset within which the value of the **Collateral** may fluctuate before triggering a right to call for cash or securities to reinstate the initial margin on the repo transaction.

Vega The change in an option's value relative to a change in the **Underlying's Volatility**.

Volatility The **Standard deviation** of the continuously compounded return on the **Underlying**. Volatility is generally annualised.

Warrant A security giving the holder a right to subscribe to a share or bond at a given price and from a certain date. If this right is not exercised before the maturity date, the warrant will expire worthless.

When-issued trading Trading a bond before the issue date; no interest is accrued during this period. Also known as the 'grey market'.

Write To sell an option is to write it. The person selling an option is known as the **Writer**.

Writer The same as 'seller' of an **Option**.

X Used to denote the strike price of an option; sometimes this is denoted using the term K.

Yield The interest rate which can be earned on an investment, currently quoted by the market or implied by the current market price for the investment – as opposed to the **Coupon** paid by an issuer on a security, which is based on the coupon rate and the face value. For a bond, generally the same as **Yield to maturity**, unless otherwise specified.

Yield curve Graphical representation of the maturity structure of interest rates, plotting yields of bonds that are all of the same class or credit quality against the maturity of the bonds.

Yield-curve option   Option that allows purchasers to take a view on a yield curve without having to take a view about a market's direction.

Yield-curve swap   Swap in which the index rates of the two interest streams are at different points on the yield curve. Both payments are refixed with the same frequency whatever the index rate.

Yield to equivalent life   The same as **Yield to maturity** for a bond with partial redemptions.

Yield to maturity   The **Internal rate of return** of a bond – the yield necessary to discount all the bond's cashflows to an **NPV** equal to its current price. *See* **Simple yield to maturity, Current yield.**

YTM   *See* **Yield to maturity.**

Zero-coupon   A zero-coupon security is one that does not pay a **Coupon**. Its price is correspondingly less to compensate for this. A zero-coupon **Yield** is the yield which a zero-coupon investment for that term would have if it were consistent with the **Par yield curve.**

Zero-coupon bond   Bond on which no coupon is paid. It is either issued at a discount or redeemed at a premium to face value.

Zero-coupon swap   Swap converting the payment pattern of a **Zero-coupon bond**, either to that of a normal, coupon-paying fixed-rate bond or to a **Floating rate.**

ABBREVIATIONS

. . . .

ACT	Association of Corporate Treasurers
ALM	Asset & Liability Management
ATM	At-the-money
BBA	British Bankers Association
BPV	Basis Point Value
CBOT	Chicago Board of Trade
CD	Certificate of Deposit
CDS	Credit Default Swap
CGO	Central Gilts Office
CME	Chicago Mercantile Exchange
CMO	Central Moneymarkets Office
CMTM	Current Mark-To-Market
CP	Commercial Paper
CRND	Commissioners for the Reduction of the National Debt
CTD	Cheapest-To-Deliver
DBV	Delivery By Value
DMO	Debt Management Office
DVP	Delivery Versus Payment
EDSP	Exchange Delivery Settlement Price
FRA	Forward Rate Agreement
FSA	Financial Services Authority
FXA	Forward Exchange Agreement
G7	Group of Seven
GC	General Collateral
GDP	Gross Domestic Product
GEMM	Gilt-Edged Market Maker
GIC	Guaranteed Investment Contract

GNP	Gross National Product
GRY	Gross Redemption Yield
ICMA	International Capital Markets Association
IDB	Inter-Dealer Broker
IG	Index-linked Gilt
IRR	Implied Repo Rate
ISDA	International Swaps and Derivatives Association
LCH	London Clearing House
LIBID	The London Interbank BID rate
LIBOR	London Inter-Bank Offer Rate
LIFFE	London International Financial Futures Exchange
LND	Last Notice Day
LSE	London Stock Exchange
LTD	Last Trading Day
MACD	Moving Average Convergence/Divergence
MBS	Mortgage-Backed Security
NPV	Net Present Value
O/N	OverNight
OTC	Over-The-Counter
p&l	Profit & loss
REPO	Sale and repurchase agreement
RPI	Retail Price Index
RR	Reverse Repo
SAFE	Synthetic Agreement for Forward Exchange
SFA	Securities and Futures Authority
T-bond	US Treasury bond
VAR	Value-At-Risk
xd	Ex-dividend
YTM	Yield-To-Maturity

INDEX